TOAD
Pocket Reference for Oracle

TOAD
Pocket Reference for Oracle

Jim McDaniel and Patrick McGrath
Quest Software, Inc.

O'REILLY®

Beijing · Cambridge · Farnham · Köln · Paris · Sebastopol · Taipei · Tokyo

TOAD Pocket Reference for Oracle

by Jim McDaniel and Patrick McGrath
Quest Software, Inc.

Published by O'Reilly Media, Inc., 1005 Gravenstein Highway North, Sebastopol, CA 95472.

O'Reilly Media, Inc. books may be purchased for educational, business, or sales promotional use. Online editions are also available for most titles (*safari.oreilly.com*). For more information, contact our corporate/institutional sales department: (800) 998-9938 or *corporate@oreilly.com*.

Editor:	Deborah Russell
Production Editor:	Jane Ellin
Cover Designer:	Ellie Volckhausen
Interior Designer:	David Futato

Printing History:

August 2002:	First Edition

0-596-00337-4
[C]

Contents

TOAD Pocket Reference for Oracle

Foreword

My first home office contained two sawhorses and an old door that I used as a computer desk for my 286 computer. It was from that office that I first began writing TOAD for my own use on Oracle assignments. I had no idea then that TOAD would eventually become what it is today. Some have labeled TOAD a phenomenon and classify the TOADies as a cult following. To me, TOAD is still just "my baby," and despite the growth of the TOAD Team from one person to nine, we continue to do things in the same interactive, and sometimes reactive, manner that has been our history.

Developing TOAD over the years has been—and continues to be—great fun for me. I enjoy the regular contact with "my" users, many of whom I now consider close personal friends. And I especially appreciate the TOAD Team. They are a small band of dedicated and stellar professionals who have pushed the product much further than I could have done alone.

There are currently more than 200,000 registered users of both the commercial and freeware versions of TOAD, and the product has become the dominant development environment in the Oracle space. I would like to thank the TOAD user community for their enthusiastic and loyal support of both the product and me. I hope we will have the same fun together for many years to come.

– Jim McDaniel (the TOADman)

Introduction

This book is a quick reference designed to help Oracle end users (data analysts, developers, designers, DBAs, etc.) become better users of TOAD (the Tool for Oracle Application Developers). It is aimed at both beginning and experienced users. Clearly, given its small size, this book is not intended to be a comprehensive user's guide. Rather, it is a concise summary, designed to provide you with:

- A summary of the core functionality and major standard features available in TOAD
- A handy quick reference to TOAD's common commands and shortcut keys, as well as recommended changes to default options
- A summary of helpful TOAD usage hints, tips, and cautionary notes

The material presented here applies to both the commercial and freeware versions of the TOAD product.

TOAD is a constantly evolving product. It has had several upgrades each year since 1995. At the time this pocket reference went to press, the current version of TOAD was Version 7.4. To be useful to as many TOAD users as possible, this book focuses more on the continuing core functionality of the product than on new enhancements.

For more information about TOAD go to:

http://www.quest.com

For more information about this book, go to:

http://www.oreilly.com/catalog/tdpr

Contributors

This book is a collaborative effort involving many individuals and groups, including the TOADman, the dedicated members of the TOAD Team, the TOAD user community, and various resources at Quest Software, Inc. and O'Reilly & Associates, Inc.:

The TOADman

Without the tireless efforts of the TOADman over the past six years, TOAD, and consequently this book, would not be possible. Jim McDaniel is one of the rare software developers who actively and continually communicates with his install base to produce new features and product upgrades.

The TOAD Team

The TOADman's initial efforts on TOAD have been nearly eclipsed by those of his small band of developers, QA professionals, and tech writers. The entire team has taken on the TOAD persona and adopted the TOAD work ethic, elevating TOAD to cult status within the Oracle community.

Patrick McGrath

Patrick was responsible for providing, compiling, and editing most of the technical content in this book. He is a Senior Systems Consultant with Quest Software, Inc. Last year he served as a technical editor of *Oracle9i Development By Example* (Que Publishing).

Bert Scalzo

Bert was the main technical reviewer of this book, and we are grateful for the content he supplied. He is a software architect for Quest Software, Inc., responsible for designing a number of product features, including many of those found in the TOAD-DBA module.

Thanks as well to the O'Reilly editorial and production team, to Cam White, and to others too numerous to mention who helped bring this book to life.

Caveats

This book assumes that you have a baseline familiarity with Oracle, PL/SQL, and SQL*Plus as well as a basic understanding of Windows. In more advanced sections (e.g., "TOAD Database Administration"), we assume that you are a very experienced Oracle user.

We can't cover every possible TOAD function in this pocket reference, but we do touch upon the key functions and windows available from every major section of the main TOAD menus. There are a number of standard (and, for the most part, self-explanatory) TOAD functions that we won't mention because of space limitations. In addition, a full description of TOAD's add-on modules is beyond the scope of this small book; however, we do touch upon several optional features—for example, the extended SQL Tuning Lab, and the Knowledge Xpert programs—in the final section of this book.

For Help with TOAD

In addition to this pocket reference, there are a number of other helpful TOAD documentation resources available:

TOAD Help files
> TOAD has very complete Help files, covering every aspect of the product. Use the F1 key to access context-sensitive help for almost every TOAD window and panel.

TOAD product documentation
> See the *TOAD User's Guide*, the *TOAD Getting Started Guide*, and other PDF files in the *TOAD\docs* folder. You will find a great deal of tutorial and reference material, and a wide range of examples, in these PDF files.

TOAD user group
> Additional help is available from the TOAD Yahoo! group; to join the group, visit *http://www.toadsoft.com* and select the Support page.

Because TOAD is a highly customizable, modular product with a history of frequent updates, both the product and the documentation change frequently. Typically, each new release provides many new features and new or enhanced functionality. Always check the *Release Notes* that are installed with each new version, as well as the "What's New" page in the Help files.

If you can't locate documentation for a particular command in the described location, search Help for that command's current default location. Note that certain features (e.g., the SQL*Loader interface) are available only in the commercial version with the add-on TOAD-DBA module activated. You can check **Help → About** to verify your TOAD version or to see which modules you have installed and licensed.

Conventions

The following conventions are used in this pocket reference:

Italic
> Used for filenames, directory names, URLs, TOAD options, and occasional emphasis

Bold
> Used for TOAD menu choices

`Constant width`
> Used for code and command examples

`Constant width italic`
> Indicates that the item (e.g., a filename) is to be replaced by a user-specified value

→
> Used to indicate a menu choice; for example, **View → Options** indicates that you select View and then choose Options from the drop-down list

 (icon)
> Indicates a button available from a TOAD toolbar that is discussed in the text

TOAD Basics

What is TOAD? TOAD is a development environment for Oracle. It is a feature-rich program that provides a graphical user interface to the Oracle database. Using TOAD will make you a more productive developer or DBA. The product makes program development faster and easier, and it simplifies database administration.

This section summarizes basic guidelines for using TOAD and performing initial setup. For detailed installation instructions, consult the TOAD documentation.

Note the following TOAD basics:

- In TOAD, Oracle rules. TOAD never violates, restricts, or enhances the Oracle privileges and permissions that have been defined for you. TOAD does not affect your defined relationship to your Oracle instance in any way.

- TOAD is closely integrated with Oracle. Nearly everything you can do with Oracle's SQL*Plus you can do via TOAD.

- TOAD has numerous window- and panel-specific right mouse menus. If you anticipate additional functionality that is not apparent on the toolbar or window, try right-clicking on the mouse to see if a right mouse menu is available.

Expanding TOAD's Functionality

Once you've installed TOAD, you can choose whether or not to expand its normal functionality. You do this by running the various scripts listed in this section at setup or at an appropriate later time.

All of these scripts are stored in the *TOAD\temps* folder and they all create database objects. Some of them require DBA authority. You will need to load the selected script in

---

TOAD's SQL Editor for examination by your DBA or another administrator before executing it.

The following scripts allow you to create, save, and recall Oracle explain plans (see the discussion of explain plans later in the "SQL Tuning" section):

NOTOAD.SQL
> Creates the required database objects in the connected schema. If you choose to use this script, it will need to be run individually by each TOAD user.

TOADPREP.SQL
> Creates a central, shared TOAD schema to own the required database objects (via public grants and synonyms). Unlike *NOTOAD.SQL*, this script needs to be run only once for the entire database. We strongly advise you to create a central, shared TOAD schema that will own, monitor, and maintain all of the required TOAD database objects.

You can also run the following scripts at setup time:

TOADSECURITY.SQL
> Enables a specialized TOAD utility for limiting the ability of some TOAD users to access selected TOAD features. This script requires that the TOAD schema exist in the database.

TOADPROFILER.SQL
> Enables TOAD to work with the Oracle Probe API available with Oracle8*i* and Oracle9*i* and implemented by Oracle's DBMS_PROFILER package. (See the later section "Using the Procedure Editor.")

TOADMONITORING.SQL
> Creates the database objects used to track the history of the database monitor (**DBA → Database Monitor**), Unix monitor (**DBA → Unix Monitor**), space (**DBA → Tablespaces**), and I/O (**DBA → Tablespaces**). Collecting this data is scheduled via the Unix Job Scheduler,

with predefined, automated tasks for collecting and purging the history.

TOAD Startup Options

Over the years, TOAD has become a highly customizable product. Although default settings are provided for all functions, you'll often want to change these defaults to suit your own work environment. Throughout this book, we include suggestions for changes to the default TOAD options.

The following TOAD startup options can be changed at any time and take effect immediately. You may find that you need to refresh windows that are active at the time these changes are made. If a particular change does not work out for you, just reset it. We've listed the options you are most likely to want to change. For information on other options, see the TOAD documentation.

Most of the following options are available from **View** → **Options** → **StartUp**:

Startup Windows per Connection
(See also the DBA Options tab.) The default TOAD startup window is the SQL Editor. If you are doing development, you may find that this default is appropriate. However, if you're doing most of your work with stored programs, you may find the Procedure Editor to be a more useful default startup. And if you are a DBA, the Schema Browser or the Kill/Trace Session may be a better choice.

Play TOAD wave file at startup
The TOAD *.wav* file plays a "croak" when you open TOAD and when you successfully compile a stored program. You can disable the TOAD *.wav* file by unchecking this option. You can disable the croak following a stored program compile by unchecking *Notification when the compile process is complete* in **View** → **Options** → **Procedure Editor**.

Auto connect to user@database

You might want to consider enabling the *Auto connect* feature from **View** → **Options** → **Oracle**. If you do, TOAD will log in as your selected *user@database* without prompting when you open TOAD.

Confirm before closing TOAD

If you turn on the *Confirm before closing TOAD* option from **View** → **Options** → **General**, TOAD forces you to answer the prompt, "Are you sure you want to exit?" However, this option may also save you from inadvertently closing TOAD when all you intended to do was close a window.

Commit Automatically after every statement

Some users prefer to commit manually when needed, rather than have TOAD ask commit questions at the end of each TOAD session. From **View** → **Options** → **Oracle** you can configure TOAD either to AutoCommit after each statement or not AutoCommit.

Prompt for Commit when closing TOAD if AutoCommit is disabled

Consider setting this option as a precaution when the AutoCommit feature is disabled.

Check for access to DBMS_TRANSACTION to prevent unnecessary Commit reminders

Checking this option in **View** → **Options** → **StartUp** prevents unnecessary commit reminders when closing TOAD, according to the following conditions: When enabled, TOAD will check for the current user's access to Oracle's DBMS_TRANSACTION package. If the user has access, TOAD can determine whether there are actual transactions pending and can then prompt on exit only when necessary. If the user doesn't have access, the other TOAD *Prompt on Exit* options are followed.

The TOAD.ini File

The *TOAD.ini* file, located in the root TOAD folder, maintains initialization information such as:

- Your TOAD configuration and options settings
- Your TOAD/Oracle connection history
- Path information for executables used by TOAD, such as *TNSping*, SQL*Loader, and the user-defined external editor

You can either manually update the *TOAD.ini* file or enter various settings through various TOAD menu options (e.g., **View → Options**, **Edit → Editor Options**). You can safely remove *TOAD.ini* if you need to restore TOAD to its default settings.

TOAD Menu Toolbar

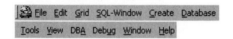

Figure 1. TOAD Menu toolbar

The TOAD Menu toolbar (shown in Figure 1) currently has the following 12 menus:

File

Provides commands to open, save, and reopen files; connect and test TOAD connections to Oracle; and perform FTP and network utility operations.

Edit

Provides both standard text-editing commands and Oracle-specific commands (e.g., Columns Dropdown). This menu works with all three TOAD editors, although the Oracle features are disabled for the offline Text Editor.

Grid

Interacts with the **SQL-Window → Results Panel → Data** tab. Provides options for searching, printing, and exporting the data displayed in the data grid.

SQL-Window

Provides options for executing, saving, and recalling SQL statements, as well as an option to execute the SQL window via SQL*Plus.

Create

Provides commands that open dialogs to create Oracle objects such as DB links, jobs, materialized views, users, etc.

Database

Repeats several commands from the TOAD Standard toolbar for opening the SQL Editor, the SQL Modeler, and the Procedure Editor, as well as providing commit and rollback functions. This menu has options for database import and export.

Tools

Contains a wide array of options including SGA/Trace Optimization, Spool SQL, TKPROF Interface, etc. It also provides several estimate and analyze utilities.

View

Provides an Explain Plan utility and a variety of reports and options. You can also open a DBMS_OUTPUT window, and perform a variety of other operations from this menu.

DBA

Provides access to a number of utilities, including monitoring options, Kill/Trace Session capabilities, expanded Export/Import utilities, etc.

Debug

Interacts with the Procedure Editor to support a full set of PL/SQL debugging tools. You can set and manipulate watches and breakpoints, use various code execution options, and so on.

Window

Provides standard window commands such as Tile Vertical and Cascade, but also displays all of your active windows in TOAD. You can navigate to any displayed window by clicking on its name.

Help

Provides access to TOAD Help, as well as links to support at Quest Software, Inc., and to the TOAD mailing lists.

The Menu toolbar, like all of the main toolbars in TOAD, is configurable. Right-click over it and choose *Customize* to arrange the TOAD Menu toolbar to best reflect how you want to work.

TOAD toolbars can also configure themselves to how you work with TOAD. If you choose the **Customize → Options → Menus** *show recently used commands first* option, then, as you work, TOAD collects usage data on the commands you use most often. Menus then personalize themselves to your work habits, moving the most used commands closer to the top of the list, and hiding commands that you rarely use.

TOAD Standard Toolbar

Figure 2. TOAD Standard toolbar

The TOAD Standard toolbar (shown in Figure 2) displays at the top of TOAD's main window. Options available from this toolbar range from opening the SQL Window to toggling PL/SQL profiling. The Standard toolbar displays even when TOAD is not connected to Oracle. As you would expect, most of the buttons are inactive when you are offline; however, you can open the Text Editor, configure TOAD options, or add external tools to the Standard toolbar while offline.

NOTE

In addition to customizing the menus and toolbars, you can also create your own toolbar specifically for your Oracle needs. Right-click over the Standard toolbar, select **Customize → Toolbars → New**, and then name and build your personal toolbar.

Be aware that new menu options and toolbar buttons in new TOAD releases will not automatically appear on customized menus or toolbars. However, you can add the new features by customizing the menus with the new options. You can also delete or rename the *toolbars.ini* file in the TOAD folder in order to restore default toolbar settings.

SQL Editor

The SQL Editor is one of three editors available in TOAD (the others are the Procedure Editor and the Text Editor, described later). The SQL Editor is a full-featured editor. It is generally compliant with Windows standards and is designed especially for working with Oracle databases and writing code for Oracle. With the SQL Editor, you can perform a variety of standard editing operations and TOAD-specific operations. The SQL Editor allows you to:

- Create new statements
- Edit existing files/scripts
- Drag-and-drop table names and column names into the editor

- Execute single statements, entire scripts, or selected statements in a script
- Describe tables, views, and stored programs
- Open a SQL*Plus window
- Generate explain plans
- Trace execution statistics
- Reuse previously executed SQL statements
- Format code

TOAD also allows you to designate an external editor, such as Microsoft Word, to interact with TOAD. If you choose to use such an editor, you can swap out the text from the TOAD SQL Editor to the external editor, edit the text, and then bring the results back into TOAD. (Refer to the "View › Options › Editors" section for more information.)

TOAD opens the SQL Editor by configurable default when connecting to Oracle. (Startup choices are listed under **View → Options → StartUp**.) You can also use the "Open a new SQL window" button, which is the first button on the TOAD Standard toolbar, to open the SQL Editor or to open multiple SQL Editors.

All of your Oracle user privileges, permissions, and objects are available to you in the SQL Editor, just as they are in SQL*Plus. You can type anything you want in the SQL Editor, just as you can in SQL*Plus, but execution is governed by your Oracle permissions.

The SQL Editor can handle stored programs (e.g., procedures, functions, triggers, packages, and package bodies). The SQL Editor can call these programs from an anonymous PL/SQL block; however, for editing stored procedures, you should use TOAD's Procedure Editor. The Procedure Editor provides a specialized editor with options especially appropriate for stored programs. These include compilation, execution, easy reuse of previously entered arguments, and so on. The Procedure Editor also contains default templates for procedures, functions, triggers, and packages. See the "Procedure Editor" section for details.

SQL Editor Options

TOAD's many customizable options have an impact on both the SQL Editor and overall TOAD/Oracle performance. Such options include choices of background processing, keyword highlighting, processing statements in threads, polling for DBMS output, and more.

There are three major sets of TOAD editing options, each accessed independently:

View → Options → SQL Editor
> (Or click on the Options button on the main toolbar.) These options affect only the SQL Editor.

View → Options → Editors
> (Or click on the Options button on the main toolbar.) These options affect features in all three TOAD editors: the SQL Editor, the Procedure Editor, and the Text Editor.

Edit → Editor Options
> These options are also accessible by selecting **SQL Editor → Right Mouse → Editor Options**.[*] These options also affect all three TOAD editors.

The options that we recommend you modify are described briefly in the following sections. Many other options are available; consult the TOAD documentation for details.

View → Options → SQL Editor

To get the most out of TOAD, we recommend that you make the following changes to the default settings for **View →**

---

[*] Note that in certain cases we show "Right Mouse" in a menu choice. This means that you should right-click on the mouse to see the choices.

Options → SQL Editor. You can easily reset these options if they turn out to be inappropriate for your work environment.

Process statements in threads/allow queries to be canceled
Turn this setting on (the default is off). The Cancel button on the main Edit toolbar then becomes active when processing long-running statements.

# of SQL statements to save
Change this number from 100 (the default) to 999. TOAD keeps a running record of the SQL statements executed in the SQL Editor in the *SQLS.dat* file. This file is stored in your local TOAD folder and is maintained between sessions.

Make Code Format
Verify that this format matches the coding language you are currently using: Visual Basic (the default), Java, C++, or Perl. This setting automatically sets the coding language for *Strip Code Statement*.

Always show statement execution time (overrides ROW-COL display)
Turn this setting on (the default is off).

Prompt to save contents when closing editor
Consider turning on this setting (the default is off). You will need to balance the benefit of safeguarding your work against the inconvenience of having to answer the "Do you want to save it first?" question.

NOTE

You can locate options by searching on keywords like "columns" via the dialog box at the bottom of the **View → Options** window.

View → Options → Editors

The settings under **View → Options → Editors** apply primarily to the SQL Editor and the Procedure Editor (not all of

---

the options are appropriate for the Text Editor). Review the available options and choose the settings that are appropriate for your own working environment.

Show Views on Table Selector
> Turn this setting on (the default is off) if you work regularly with views. It provides an easy method to drag existing views into the SQL Editor, the Procedure Editor, and the SQL Modeler. (The SQL Modeler is described briefly in the "SQL Modeler" section.)

Show Synonyms on Table Selector
> Turn this setting on (the default is off) if you work regularly with synonyms. It provides an easy method to drag existing synonyms into the SQL Editor, the Procedure Editor, and the SQL Modeler. If you have a significant number of synonyms, consider applying filters in the Schema Browser (described in the "Schema Browser" section) to limit the range of synonyms being loaded.

External Editor Command line
> If you need to use an external editor (such as Microsoft Word) in addition to the three TOAD editors, you need to configure TOAD to launch that editor when necessary. Enter the full path for that editor in the *External Editor Command Line* textbox and put a %S after it. TOAD can then launch that editor from the SQL Editor window and load any text present in the SQL Editor into the designated external editor. (See the discussion of the external editor in the "Text Editor" section.)

Click OK to set the options. Note that currently active windows may need to be refreshed before they reflect the changes you have made.

Edit → Editor Options

The settings under **Edit → Editor Options** affect all three TOAD editors: the SQL Editor, the Procedure Editor, and the Text Editor. This set of options is also accessible via **SQL Editor → Right Mouse → Editor Options**.

There are five groups of options:

> General Options
> Highlighting
> Key Assignments
> Auto Replace
> Code Templates

Within General Options, there are four categories: Printing Options, Display Options, Control Options, and General Options.

We recommend that you change the following settings:

Display Line numbers in gutter
> Available from **General Options → Display Options**. Turn on this setting. It takes effect in all TOAD editors. Even the CALL STACK displayed in the Procedure Editor reflects the text line number in the editor. This option counts blank and commented lines.

Printing Options
> Available from **General Options → Printing Options**. Review the settings of these options to consider adding time stamping, line numbering, and source file location to your SQL Editor printout.

Auto Replace
> Review the settings for these options as well. Auto Replace is a customizable type-ahead function—basically, a text string replacement tool that can be used to correct typos and provide typing shortcuts.

Code Templates
> Review the settings for these options, along with each of the default code templates, and consider their usefulness in writing uniform code. Also consider creating templates and importing existing scripts to use as code templates.

SQL Editor Display

The SQL Editor normally displays an upper Editing panel and a lower multi-tabbed Results panel (use of this panel is described later in the "Using the Results Panel" section). A toggle button located between the two panels allows you to toggle a full-screen display of the SQL Editor. In addition to the toggle button, you can use these keys:

F2
> To toggle a full-screen Editing panel

SHIFT-F2
> To toggle a full-screen Results panel

SQL Editor Toolbars and Menus

The SQL Editor contains an extensive set of commands with multiple launch points, including menus, toolbars, shortcut keys, and right mouse menus. In general, with the SQL Editor you can edit text and execute statements from the Edit and SQL-Window menus.

In addition to TOAD's Standard toolbar at the top of the window, there are two specialized Edit toolbars: the main SQL Edit toolbar and the Standard (or Common) Edit toolbar. The Standard Edit toolbar appears in the SQL Editor, the Procedure Editor, and the Text Editor. The SQL Editor window also has an extensive right mouse menu. We'll briefly describe the features of the various TOAD editing menus in the following sections.

TOAD editing commands can be executed from several different locations in order to accommodate different user orientations (some users prefer the mouse, others the keyboard; some like toolbars, others like menus). For instance, you can execute a single SQL statement by pressing F9, by selecting the Execute Statement icon on the Edit toolbar, or by selecting *Execute SQL All* from the SQL Editor pull-down menu.

SQL Editor: SQL Edit toolbar

The SQL Edit toolbar is the middle of the three toolbars displayed in the SQL Editor. (The others are the TOAD Standard toolbar and the Standard Edit toolbar.) It contains buttons for executing statements and scripts, recalling previous SQL, generating explain plans, and more. This toolbar also displays a Cancel button for long-running queries.

The SQL Edit toolbar is configurable. To change your options, select **Right Mouse** → **Customize** from the toolbar. Then follow the instructions to add or remove buttons.

SQL Editor: Standard Edit toolbar

The Standard (Common) Edit toolbar is at the top of the SQL Editor window and is also customizable. This toolbar is common to the SQL Editor and the Procedure Editor. It also appears in a somewhat modified fashion in the Text Editor. Standard editing features, such as cut, copy, paste, search, search and replace, undo, etc., are located here and should be self-explanatory.

SQL-Window menu

The SQL-Window menu (shown in Figure 3) available from the SQL Editor shares certain SQL execution options with the SQL Edit toolbar; for example, you can execute a single SQL statement, a highlighted statement, or an entire script. In addition to executing the current contents of the SQL-Window, the menu also lets you recall and reuse previously executed SQL statements.

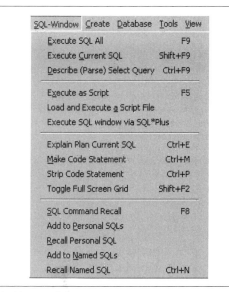

SQL-Window	Create	Database	Tools	View
Execute SQL All				F9
Execute Current SQL				Shift+F9
Describe (Parse) Select Query				Ctrl+F9
Execute as Script				F5
Load and Execute a Script File				
Execute SQL window via SQL*Plus				
Explain Plan Current SQL				Ctrl+E
Make Code Statement				Ctrl+M
Strip Code Statement				Ctrl+P
Toggle Full Screen Grid				Shift+F2
SQL Command Recall				F8
Add to Personal SQLs				
Recall Personal SQL				
Add to Named SQLs				
Recall Named SQL				Ctrl+N

Figure 3. SQL-Window menu

Edit menu

The Edit menu (shown in Figure 4) available from the TOAD Menu toolbar includes many of the usual editing features for cut, copy, paste, find, replace, and other such functions. The Edit menu also provides a number of Oracle features for describing the object at the cursor, displaying a column name list for the table or view at the cursor, and displaying procedure arguments. It also provides an alias replacement function and many other functions.

SQL Editor → Right Mouse menu

Select the **SQL Editor → Right Mouse menu** to access additional text-editing and SQL execution commands. Using this menu (shown in Figure 5), you can set bookmarks for easy navigation through long scripts. You can also change blocks

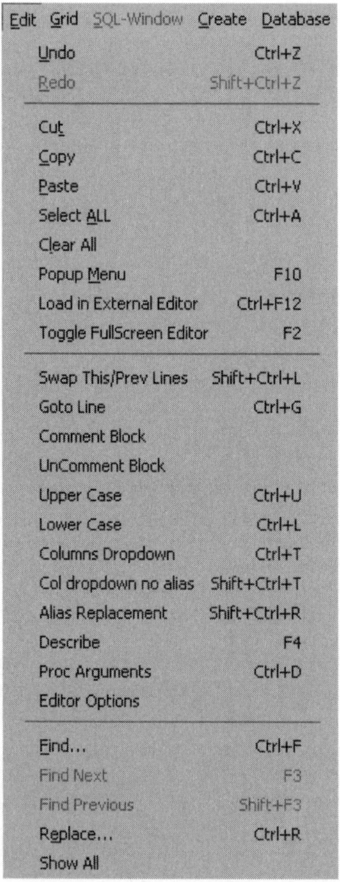

Figure 4. TOAD Edit menu

to all uppercase or lowercase or capitalize the first letter of
each word. *Comment Block* and *UnComment Block* options
are also available, as are options to create PL/SQL's DBMS_
OUTPUT statements, apply Unix-style file saves, select the

desired Oracle optimizer mode, and initiate Oracle's SQL Trace (TKPROF) and TOAD's AutoTrace programs in order to gather Oracle execution statistics.

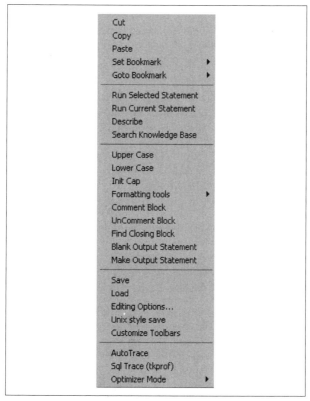

Figure 5. SQL Editor right mouse menu

SQL Editor Shortcut Keys

The SQL Editor provides a set of shortcut keys that you can use instead of selecting options from the various editing menus. Table 1 lists all available keys.

Table 1. SQL Editor shortcut keys

Shortcut key	Function
F1	Windows Help for current window
F2	Toggle full-screen Editing panel
SHIFT-F2	Toggle full-screen Results panel
F3	Find next occurrence
SHIFT-F3	Find previous occurrence
F4	Describe highlighted table, view, procedure, function, or package in pop-up window
F5	Execute as script
F6	Toggle active window between SQL Editor and Results panel
	Clear all text in SQL Editor, Data tab, and Explain Plan tab
F8	Recall previous SQL statement in SQL Editor (full history view)
F9	Execute statement in SQL Editor
CTRL-F9	Verify SELECT statement without execution (parse) in SQL Editor
SHIFT-F9	Execute statement at cursor in SQL Editor
F10	Pop-up menu
CTRL-F12	Load in external editor
CTRL-A	Select all text
CTRL-C	Copy

Table 1. SQL Editor shortcut keys (continued)

Shortcut key	Function
CTRL-E	Execute explain plan on the statement or on the highlighted statement
CTRL-F	Find text
CTRL-G	Go to line number
CTRL-L	Convert highlighted text to lowercase
CTRL-M	Make code statement
CTRL-N	Recall named SQL statement
CTRL-O	Open a file for editing
CTRL-P	Strip code statement
CTRL-R	Find and replace
CTRL-S	Save file
SHIFT-CTRL-S	Save file as
CTRL-T	Column drop-down for highlighted table, view, or synonym
CTRL-U	Convert highlighted text to uppercase
CTRL-V	Paste
CTRL-X	Cut
CTRL-Z	Undo last change
SHIFT-CTRL-Z	Redo last undo
ALT-UP	Display previously executed statement (single statement view)
ALT-DOWN	Display next statement (after ALT-UP in single statement view)
CTRL-HOME	In the data grids, go to the top of the record set
CTRL-END	In the data grids, go to the end of the record set
CTRL-TAB	Cycle through the open windows in TOAD
CTRL-ENTER	Execute current SQL (same as F9)
CTRL-(period)	Auto-complete table name, view, or synonym after initial character(s) have been typed

TOAD allows you to customize shortcut keys in the SQL Editor, Procedure Editor, and Text Editor. To do so, you need to change the *plsqlkeys.bin* file in the *TOAD\temps* folder. However, you must not edit this file directly. Make all file modifications by selecting **Edit → Editor Options → Key Assignments**.

As we mentioned, some menu options and toolbar buttons do not have a predefined shortcut key. You can customize additional shortcut keys in TOAD by right-clicking over the TOAD Standard toolbar and choosing *Menu Shortcuts*.

Supporting Other Parsers/Languages

While the SQL Editor supports only Oracle's own PL/SQL language, the Procedure Editor and the Text Editor can parse text from other languages such as HTML and Java. These editors recognize the language you are using by the extension of the file that is loaded.

Go to **View → Options → Parser Scripts** to configure support for other languages. To configure options for TOAD's parser scripts, go to **Edit → Editor Options**.

The filenames for the parser of a given language (e.g., HTML) all start with the name of that language (e.g., *htmlscr.txt, htmlkeys.bin, htmlopts.txt, html.dci*).

Opening Files in the SQL Editor

There are several ways to open a file in the SQL Editor:

File → Open file
> You can open an existing file located in your Windows network via this command from the TOAD Menu toolbar.

> You can click on the "Load File into the Editor" button on the Standard Edit toolbar.

SQL Editor → Right Mouse → Load
> You can select this command from the right mouse menu.

CTRL-O
> You can type this key in any editor.

NOTE

File → Reopen File provides quick access to the previous eight files you opened in TOAD's SQL Editor, Procedure Editor, or Text Editor. The Reopen File list is common to all three editors.

Source Control in the SQL Editor and Procedure Editor

TOAD provides source control, or version control, for your files via the Procedure Editor (described in the later "Procedure Editor" section). Although source control settings don't typically affect your work in the SQL Editor, it's something you may want to be aware of as you open files.

You can check out or check in files from Microsoft Visual SourceSafe, PVCS, and other programs, provided that the client portion of the source code control install has been set up on your PC. While not all source code control (SCC)–compliant products have necessarily been tested, all such products should theoretically work with TOAD.

Make the appropriate entries in **View → Options → Source Control** so TOAD recognizes your installed version control software. You will need to provide TOAD with the path to your version control working folder. You also need to set the options for prompting for check in and check out, and for commenting when new files are added.

Using FTP and Other Networking Utilities with TOAD

TOAD's FTP utility is available from **File → FTP**. This utility does not load a file directly into the SQL Editor; however, you can use it to load files from, and save files to, your Unix servers or other accessible FTP sites. Go to **File → FTP** and click on the Connect button. You will be prompted for the host, username, and password. You can either use the navigation buttons or drag-and-drop files from the source to the target.

Once you have FTPed your script to the appropriate target folder, you can open it in the SQL Editor, the Procedure Editor, or the Text Editor, or access it via any of the TOAD file open commands.

NOTE

The radio buttons at the bottom of the FTP dialog need to be adjusted to the appropriate ASCII or binary setting for your file. There are also options under **View → Options → Network Utilities** that determine whether ASCII or binary mode will be used, based on the extension of the file to be FTPed.

File → Network Utilities also gives you access to other networking utilities. Through this menu you can telnet to another session, execute *rexec* commands, ping servers, use *TNSping*, and check the IP addresses for a hostname/URL. Each utility is available from a separate tab.

Using the TOAD Describe Facility

The TOAD Describe facility opens an extended describe for a table, view, procedure, function, package, or package body. It provides much more detailed output than does the SQL*Plus Describe command.

The TOAD Describe opens a multi-tabbed window that displays the schema name, column names, data type, data, grants, script, etc., for the described object. You can drag-and-drop column name(s) into the SQL Editor from this window. Double-clicking on the column name generates a comma-separated list. You can also check Oracle's currently enforced referential integrity, the current status of constraints and triggers, and the current data. You can also see the other Oracle objects (views, snapshots, procedures, etc.) that use the described object by clicking the appropriate tab.

You can execute the TOAD Describe by typing:

```
DESC objectname F9
```

The TOAD Describe has a predefined shortcut key: F4. Simply press F4 while your cursor rests on the object name.

NOTE

TOAD Describe is actually the Object Details panel from the Schema Browser (see the "Schema Browser" section later in this book).

SQL Editor Windows

The following sections briefly describe the characteristics of the various SQL Editor windows you can open from the Standard Edit toolbar. (These are also available in the Procedure Editor.)

Show TABLE Select window (from Standard Edit toolbar)

The Show TABLE Select window lets you display all of the table, view, and synonym names for a schema.

Click on the "Show TABLE Select Window" button at the right end of the Standard Edit toolbar. Select the appropriate schema from the list generated, and the schema objects will load. Locate the desired table, view, or synonym (listed alphabetically) on the appropriate tab. You can drag-and-drop any item from the list into the SQL Editor or the Procedure Editor. (Finding the item in the list verifies that the object currently exists in the database, and helps eliminate misspellings.) Double-click on the object name to paste it in the SQL Editor at your cursor position.

If you select or double-click on multiple object names, TOAD will build a comma-separated list starting at your cursor position in the SQL Editor.

NOTE

Views and synonyms are displayed only after you've turned on their related *Show* option in the **View** → **Options** → **Editors** panel. If you have applied filters to display or suppress objects in the Schema Browser, that filtering will apply to the Show TABLE Select window.

Show COLUMN Name Select window (from Standard Edit toolbar)

Clicking on the "Show Column Select Window" button on the far right of the Standard Edit toolbar opens the Show COLUMN Name Select window.

Select the appropriate schema from the displayed list, and then click on the radio button for tables or views. From here, you may drag-and-drop the displayed column names. (Finding the item in the list verifies that the object currently exists in the database, and helps eliminate misspellings.) The Show COLUMN Name Select window also displays the datatype, indicates Null or Not Null, and shows the default value for each column.

This window does not have an option to display detailed column information for a synonym. For synonyms, you will have to use the TOAD Describe facility in the SQL Editor.

SQL Template window (from Standard Edit toolbar)

The "Show SQL Template window" button is the last button on the far right of the Standard Edit toolbar.

Clicking on this button brings up the SQL Templates window. A series of drop-down lists displays Oracle date, group, and single-row character functions, and single-row number functions. The SQL Template window is divided into upper and lower panels; functions are listed in the upper panel, and the description of the highlighted function is displayed in the lower panel. You can drag the displayed functions directly into the SQL Editor. You can also use the Direct button at the bottom of the screen to paste them into the SQL Editor.

You can customize all of the function lists displayed in this window by editing the appropriate *FUNCS.TXT* files in the *TOAD\temps* folder. There is a specific section for your own SQL templates labeled User Provided Function List, which you can populate by editing the *USRFUNCS.TXT* file in the *TOAD\temps* folder.

Executing SQL with the SQL Editor

This section describes the SQL Editor commands that allow you to execute SQL statements: single statements, multiple statements, and entire scripts.

SQL-Window → Execute Statement/Execute SQL All (executing a single statement)

You can use the SQL Editor to execute a variety of SQL statements, including SELECT, UPDATE, INSERT, DELETE, DROP, etc. To execute a single statement, type it in the SQL Editor; for example:

```
SELECT * FROM tablename WHERE ROWNUM < 50
```

If you omit the concluding semicolon at the end of the statement, the SQL Editor will add it if necessary before executing the statement.

There are several other ways to execute a SQL statement. You can select **SQL-Window → Execute SQL All**, click on the "Execute Statement" button on the SQL Edit toolbar, or press F9. Your execution results will display on the Data tab in the Results panel (see the "Using the Results Panel" section).

SQL-Window → Execute as Script (executing multiple statements and scripts)

You can also use the SQL Editor to execute a series of SQL
statements. As with single-statement execution, there are various ways to execute a series of statements. You can click on
 the "Execute as Script" button from the Standard Edit toolbar, select **SQL-Window** → **Execute as Script**, or press F5.
Execution begins with the first statement and continues
through the statements in order. If TOAD encounters an
error, it will ask you if you want to continue or terminate the
script.

The output from a series of statements or a script is spooled
to the Script Output tab in the Results panel; the Data tab is
not populated. Note that you cannot manipulate the resulting data sets on the Script Output tab as you can the data
available on the Data tab.

Script output is available only in read-only mode. You can
print it, save it to a file or to the clipboard, and paste it into
any editor.

Cancel running statement (from SQL Edit Toolbar)

TOAD lets you cancel long-running queries (executing on
Oracle8 or higher versions). First, you must verify that the
option **View** → **Options** → **SQL Editor** → **Process Statements**

in threads/allow queries to be canceled has been set. When a statement such as the following is executed:

```
SELECT * FROM DBA_OBJECTS ORDER BY object_id
```

the Cancel button at the right end of the SQL Edit toolbar becomes active for as long as the query can be terminated.

Change Active Sessions for this Window (from SQL Edit toolbar)

TOAD supports multiple simultaneous connections to the same (or different) Oracle instances with the same (or different) Oracle logins. When you need to execute a statement or a script on an Oracle instance that's different from the one you are currently connected to, or if you wish to run it as a different owner, click on the "Change Active Session for this Window" button at the far right on TOAD's Standard toolbar. If you already have other TOAD sessions active, they display, along with the option to open a new session. The new session opens at your current active window instead of using your default startup window.

NOTE

When you click on the "Change Active Session for this Window" button, you can navigate between your current session and your new session. TOAD displays your login name and your instance name at the top and at the bottom of each window.

SQL-Window → Execute SQL window via SQL*Plus

The SQL Editor can execute many of Oracle's SQL*Plus commands; however, some SQL*Plus commands are either ignored or not supported. If your SQL contains SQL*Plus commands that are not supported in the SQL Editor (see the upcoming note), select **SQL-Window → Execute SQL window via SQL*Plus**. TOAD opens a SQL*Plus connection in an independent window using your current TOAD/Oracle login. Your SQL will be executed immediately without further prompting.

You can then arrange your desktop to take advantage of the SQL Editor for editing statements or full scripts and copy and paste them into the SQL*Plus window.

NOTE

Remember to add the final semicolon (;) before attempting to execute TOAD's SQL Editor window in SQL*Plus.

Search on SQL*Plus in TOAD Help for the list of SQL*Plus commands currently supported by the SQL Editor.

Make/Strip Code Statement (from SQL Edit toolbar)

The "Make Code Statement" and "Strip Code Statement" buttons let you add development code syntax to SQL statements (Make Code) or remove it from these statements (Strip Code). These buttons are located on the SQL Edit toolbar.

With a single, valid SQL statement in the SQL Editor, or a highlighted statement and the appropriate code development language (Delphi, VB, C++, Java, or Perl) selected in **View → Options → SQL Editors**, click on the "Make Code Statement" button (the first one labeled VB). Alternately, use the CTRL-M command. This adds the development code to your statement and copies it to the clipboard. TOAD displays an appropriate message, such as "Java statement copied to the clipboard," in the status bar at the bottom of the SQL Editor.

To reverse the action and remove development code from your statement, copy the SQL from your development code into the SQL Editor. Then highlight it and click on the second VB button on the SQL Edit toolbar. Alternately, use the CTRL-P command.

TOAD EDIT command

As an alternative to executing an updateable SQL command, consider using a TOAD EDIT command such as the following when you need to update, insert, or delete data for a table:

```
EDIT tablename F9
```

This command is the equivalent of running:

```
SELECT tablename.*, ROWID FROM tablename
```

Both commands return all the data from the specified object in updateable mode. A green box displays in the status indicator panel at the bottom of the window. A green status indicator means that you are in Updateable mode. The Data Edit buttons ("Insert a row," "Delete a row," "Post data changes," and "Revert data changes") on the SQL Edit toolbar also become active.

Additional SQL Editor Features

In addition to providing such standard editing commands as search-and-replace, indent blocks, undo, and redo last undo, the SQL Editor supports a number of unique features, which are described in the following sections.

Edit → Column Dropdown

As we saw earlier, TOAD can display a list of columns for a table or a view. Type the object name in the SQL Editor and follow it with either a period or a CTRL-T command, as follows:

```
tablename.
tablename CTRL-T
```

The Column Dropdown list is also available as a menu item. Position your cursor at the desired table name and select **Edit → Column Dropdown**. You can select column names from the displayed list.

SQL-Window → SQL Command Recall

By default, the previous 100 SQL statements executed in the SQL Editor are saved in the *SQLS.dat* file in your local TOAD folder. You can display a list of your available statements by pressing F8, selecting **SQL-Window → SQL Command Recall**, or clicking the "Recall Previous SQL" button on the Standard Edit toolbar. SQL statements are listed in most recently used order. The *SQLS.dat* file is maintained between TOAD sessions, and the older statements age out as you continue to execute new statements.

The SQL Statement Recall window has various operation buttons at the top of the screen. These buttons let you navigate through the list and select and delete statements from it. There is also a *SQL Contains* search available from this window. When you enter a text string, the *Go* command just to the right of the dialog box becomes active. When you are searching for a SQL statement with a unique text string in it, use the SQL Contains dialog to filter out all of the statements that don't contain that text string.

When you locate the desired statement, you can use the "Editor Append" or "Editor Replace" buttons to paste the SQL into the SQL Editor. Double-clicking the desired statement also replaces all the text in the editor unless you set the option under **View → Options → SQL Editor → Appends Rather than Replaces**.

NOTE

Clicking the "Editor Replace" button immediately replaces all of the contents of the SQL Editor. This button overrides the modified *Appends Rather than Replaces* option setting described above.

SQL-Window → Recall Named SQL/Recall Personal SQL

The Recall Personal SQL and Recall Named SQL functions are logical extensions of the SQL Command Recall command. The major difference is that with these commands you get to choose which statements get saved:

Recall Named SQL
> Creates the file *NAMEDSQL.dat* in your *TOAD\temps* folder. This file gives you the ability to associate a SQL statement with a logical name for quick reference.

Recall Personal SQL
> Creates the file *PERSSQLS.dat* in your TOAD folder.

Both functions include all of the functionality found in SQL Command Recall. While TOAD does check for previous usage of the same name when you select **SQL-Window → Add to Named SQLs**, TOAD does not check for previous occurrences of the same statement at this time.

SQL-Window → Describe (Parse) Select Query

TOAD has the ability to parse a SELECT statement and report on which columns will be returned. Type any single SELECT statement, such as the following, in the SQL Editor:

```
SELECT * FROM tablename WHERE rownum < 30
```

Instead of immediately executing the statement, you can parse the statement either by pressing CTRL-F9 or by selecting the **SQL Window → Describe (Parse) Select Query** command. The resulting window displays the column names, datatypes, and data lengths of all of the columns that will be returned by the query.

If you misspell a column name, or if that column no longer exists, the query will not parse completely but will stop at the invalid column name.

Code templates

TOAD comes with approximately two dozen default code completion templates for SQL operations (e.g., entire cursor block, package spec cursor, function shell). These appear in a pop-up menu that is common to the SQL Editor, the

Procedure Editor, and the Text Editor. You can open the Code Completion Template pop-up by pressing CTRL-Spacebar. You can also bring the code into the editor by typing its shortcut followed by CTRL-Spacebar. For instance, if you type:

```
Crbl CTRL-Spacebar
```

TOAD opens the SQL template for declaring a cursor block (Crbl) in the editor. You are then prompted to enter the appropriate values.

In addition to using the default templates, you can create your own templates with positions marked for table names and other substitutions by selecting **Edit → Editor Options → Code Templates**. In addition to creating templates in the editor, you can use the "Load from File" button at the bottom of the window to load your previously defined files and formats into TOAD's code templates.

The source for TOAD's code completion templates is the *PLSQL.dci* file in your TOAD folder.

Right Mouse → Formatting → Format Code

If you have a licensed copy of Formatter Plus, TOAD lets you format the entire contents of the SQL Editor. TOAD can format a single, valid SQL statement, a series of statements, or an entire script (including comments). With your code displayed in the SQL Editor, select **Right Mouse → Formatting Tools → Format Code**.

You can customize formatting from **View → Formatting Options**.

NOTE

If your code fails to format properly, look at the SQL Editor's status bar, and check your code for syntax errors.

Edit → Comment Block/UnComment Block and Right Mouse → Comment Block/UnComment Block

TOAD provides a convenient method for adding comments to, and removing comments from, your code. These commands are available from **Edit → Comment Block** and **Edit → UnComment Block** as well as from **Right Mouse → Comment Block** and **Right Mouse → UnComment Block**. The commands are available in the SQL Editor, the Procedure Editor, and the Text Editor.

When you comment a block, TOAD comments out the highlighted section of a displayed script in the SQL Editor by adding a double dash to the beginning of each line.

Substitution variables

TOAD's SQL Editor prompts for substitution variables in a similar, but more detailed fashion than SQL*Plus. You can use either the *:columnname* or the *&columnname* format. When the statement containing the variable is executed, you are prompted to select the input datatype (i.e., string, integer, date, etc.) and then input the actual value. If you define multiple substitutions, you will need to click through all of them, providing input. Note that the SQL Editor does not force you to enter a value before executing the statement.

Using the Results Panel

As mentioned earlier, the lower half of TOAD's SQL Editor display is the multi-tabbed Results panel. The six tabs on the Results panel are:

Data
Explain Plan
Auto Trace
DBMS Output
Code Statistics (available only if you have a licensed copy of Formatter Plus)
Script Output

Some are results tabs and some are tuning tabs.

The results tabs—Data, DBMS Output, and Script Output—populate when you execute a statement or a script in the SQL Editor. Once populated, each results tab preserves its displayed contents until it is refreshed as the result of another statement's execution. For example, if you have data displayed on the Data tab and you then execute a script, the Script Output tab is populated but the Data tab continues to display the results of the previous execution.

Two of the tuning tabs, Explain Plan and Code Statistics, do not require execution to generate results. However, the Auto Trace tab is populated only when Auto Trace is enabled prior to statement execution. The tuning tabs are described in "SQL Tuning," later in the book.

The results tabs are:

Data

Data resulting from a query displays on the Data tab in a grid format. Both the Grid menu available from the TOAD Menu toolbar and the right mouse menu available from this Data tab have options for counting, sorting, and exporting the data displayed in the data grid. The later sections "Data tab and data grid" and "Editing Data in the SQL Editor's Data Grid" describe the Data tab and its data grid in greater detail.

Script Output

This tab is populated when you select **SQL-Window** → **Execute as Script** from the TOAD Menu toolbar or **Execute as a Script** from the SQL Edit toolbar. You can run this command on a single SQL statement, on multiple SQL statements, or on an entire script. The command instructs TOAD to execute each subsequent statement in sequence and to ignore commented lines. Output is spooled to the Script Output tab as execution is completed. Both the executed statement and its results are displayed. You can save or print this output, but you can't directly edit or manipulate it, as you can the results in the data grid.

DBMS Output
Output from calls to Oracle's DBMS_OUTPUT package displays in the DBMS Output tab. This output won't appear, however, unless you've clicked the "Turn Output On" button on the DBMS Output window toolbar. You also need to set the appropriate buffer size and polling interval for your anticipated output.

The Results panel tabs offer various combinations of interior toolbars and right mouse menus. You can set several options that may help maximize Results panel performance; these are described in the following sections.

Results panel: View → Options → Data Grids → Data

From **View → Options → Data Grids → Data**, you can set several options:

Close SQL cursor when exporting grid contents
Turn on this option if you anticipate exporting the data grid frequently. It generally produces faster exports and uses less memory.

Check and warn of cascading constraints before deletions
Turning on this option reduces the number of Oracle error messages you receive.

Precision for Float columns, Precision for integer columns
Review these values. Both default to zero, so you should adjust these values appropriately.

Confirm data deletions from grids
Consider turning on this option, especially for users new to Oracle.

Allow Control-J to cancel data fetches (grid scrolls)
Turn on this option. When checked, this option allows you to disable scrolling in a large data set displayed in

the data grid by typing CTRL-J. No data is fetched
beyond the point where you stopped scrolling.

NOTE

Options such as *Confirm data deletions from grids* are intended to complement, not replace, your current Oracle
privileges.

Results panel: View → Options → Data Grids → Visual

There are also a number of helpful Results panel options
available from **View → Options → Data Grids → Visual**:

Column sizing
> Review the various options for sizing columns by the
> header or data width.

Show row numbers
> You might want to turn on this option. An additional
> column will be displayed in the data grid with the related
> count information.
>
> Note that you can selectively hide the row number col-
> umn in the Results panel's Data tab by using the data
> grid's **Right Mouse → Select Columns** option.

The Data Grids options apply to many data grids in TOAD,
not only the data grid displayed on the Data tab available
from the Results panel; for example, the Data tab for tables
and views in the Schema Browser, the Query Results tab in
the SQL Modeler, and the grids in the Master/Detail
browser.

Data tab and data grid

TOAD provides a number of ways to manipulate the data
displayed in the data grid. The **Grid** menu, available from the
Toad Menu toolbar; the **Data → Right Mouse** menu, available from the Results panel; and the middle buttons on the

SQL Edit toolbar all contain commands that allow you to edit, manipulate, print, or post your changes to Oracle. Once the Data tab or data grid has been populated, you can manipulate the displayed data without having to rewrite your original SQL statement. You can search, sort, filter, or hide data in your results set. You can also change the column order by dragging the column name to a new position.

NOTE

Many of the actions involved in TOAD's manipulation of the displayed data (sorting, filtering, hiding, changing column order, etc.) take place on your PC, not within Oracle.

The data displayed in the data grid is in read-only or update-able mode depending on the type of query you ran:

Read-only
A command such as the following:

```
SELECT * FROM tablename
```

populates the data grid in read-only mode. A red box displays in the status indicator panel at the bottom of the window. A red status indicator means that you are in read-only mode. The TOAD functions for editing individual cells on the grid, adding rows, or deleting rows are all disabled when you are in read-only mode. Nevertheless, you can still search, sort, or filter data as well as change column order or hide columns in the data grid.

Updateable
A command such as the following:

```
SELECT tablename.*, ROWID FROM tablename
```

populates the data grid in updateable mode. A green box displays in the status indicator panel at the bottom of the window. A green status indicator means that you are in updateable mode. TOAD functions to edit individual cells on the grid, add rows, and delete rows are all fully enabled.

Results panel: Data → Right Mouse

A right mouse menu (shown in Figure 6) is available from the
Data tab in the Results panel.

Figure 6. Data tab right mouse menu

Most of the commands should be self-explanatory. One that
may require some clarification is Record Count, which
counts all the records returned by a query (note that this
command is not limited to counting the records displayed in
the data grid). With your data displayed in the data grid and
your cursor in the Results panel, select **Right Mouse →
Record Count**. TOAD reports your count in a TOAD Message window. While the count is running, TOAD opens a
Fetching Count window; you can cancel this operation if you
wish.

Editing Data in the SQL Editor's Data Grid

In the previous sections, we introduced the SQL Editor's Results panel and briefly described the data grid displayed from the Data tab. The following sections provide more detailed information about common data-editing operations you might want to perform on this data.

If the Results panel status indicator is green, you can type your data changes directly into the data grid. You can insert a row or delete the currently selected row using the buttons in the middle of the SQL Edit toolbar.

DATE and NUMBER cell options

Clicking on the far right of a DATE cell brings up a calendar from which you can select the date and year. Clicking in the middle of a DATE cell brings up a TIME STAMP selector for minutes, seconds, etc. Clicking on the far right of a NUMBER cell brings up a calculator.

Commit/Rollback data

Once you have made changes to the data grid, you can commit them by clicking on the Commit button on the TOAD Standard toolbar. You can also select Commit from the right mouse menu launched by clicking on *username@connected-instance* in the lower left of your TOAD window.

To roll back changes, you can click on the Rollback button (adjacent to the Commit button) or select Rollback from the right mouse menu as you would for Commit.

Single Record View (update data)

You can access the Single Record View by clicking on the book icon in the upper left of the data grid. The Single Record View window opens and displays your current record on a single panel. This view reflects any sorting and filtering of data, and any hiding or reordering of columns, that have been set in the data grid. (Sorting, filtering, and so on are described in the following sections.)

There are navigation buttons at the top of the Single Record View window for moving to First record, Prior record, Next record, and Last record.

You can insert and delete records from the Single Record View using the + and – buttons. You can then post your changes to the database. There is also a button to refresh your data after posting your changes.

Sort data (ascending and descending order)

A single left mouse click on a column header in the data grid opens a dialog to apply or remove an ascending or descending sort on that column. When the operation is complete, the data grid refreshes. A pointer displayed in the column header indicates the direction of the sort.

You can remove the sort using the same left mouse click on the column header in the data grid. If you wish, you can also remove the sort confirmation when clicking on column headers by going to **Options** → **Data Grids** → **Visual** and unchecking *Confirm sorts when clicking on column header*.

Sort data (column order)

To change the order of columns in the data grid, position your cursor on the column header for the column you wish to move. Hold down the left mouse button, drag the column to its desired position, and release. The dragged column drops to the left of the green position indicator arrows. These arrows appear on your screen when you are reordering columns.

Grid → Filter Data

With the data grid populated, select **Grid** → **Filter Data** from the TOAD Menu toolbar. The Filter Condition window builds a data filter in a point-and-click fashion. The column names from the data grid display in one panel, and a series of operators displays in another. After clicking the column names and the operators into the Filter Condition window, you can complete the filter by typing in a value directly.

As an alternative to using the point-and-click approach, you can type your desired filter (including column names and operators) directly into the Filter Condition window.

Data → Right Mouse → Select Columns

The Select Columns command lets you select which columns returned by your query should be displayed in the data grid. From the Results panel, use **Data → Right Mouse → Select Columns** to open the Select Columns window. At the bottom of that window are two buttons: "Unselect All" and "Select All." Initially, all of the columns displayed in the data grid are checked (selected). Click off the columns you want to hide and then click OK.

The Select Columns window also lets you display row numbers and, if your results are updateable, the ROWID.

Export data options

Once you have assembled, sorted, and filtered your data, numerous output options are available to you:

Flat File Export
> This command is available from both the Grid menu on the TOAD Menu toolbar and the Results panel's **Data → Right Mouse** menus. See the next section for more information on flat file exports.

Allow Multi-Select
> If you select this command from the **Data → Right Mouse** menu on the Results panel, you can follow Windows conventions to highlight the desired row(s) and then press CTRL-C to copy selected row(s) to the clipboard.

Save As

This command is available from both the Grid menu on the TOAD Menu toolbar and the **Data → Right Mouse** menu on the Results panel. The command opens the Save Grid Contents window. From there you can select the appropriate format in which to save all the data returned by your query. See the "Save As (file format)" section for more information.

Flat File Export

The Flat File Export command is available from both the TOAD Menu toolbar's Grid menu and the Result panel's **Data → Right Mouse** menus. Selecting this command opens the Flat File Export from the Query window. This window has three tabs: Options, Spec File, and SQL*Loader:

Options

Start with this tab and select either *To Clipboard* or *To File*. If you choose *To File*, the Data Filename dialog box becomes active.

You may notice that the options to select a schema or a table are grayed out on the Options tab when you are attempting a flat file export of the results from a query. These selections become active when you select *Export/ Table as Flat File* from the Database pull-down menu.

Spec File

Next, go to this tab and click on the "Generate Columns" button at the top of the window. You can also input your Spec File name via this tab; press Execute to perform the export.

*SQL*Loader*

To create a simple SQL*Loader control file that you can use to upload the exported data, select the appropriate options from this tab; specify a Badfile name and press the "Save to file" button to save the control file.

Save As (file format)

The Save As command is available from both the Grid menu on the TOAD Menu toolbar and the Results panel's **Data →
Right Mouse** menu. You can choose to save the data in the data grid in any of the following formats: ASCII, Comma Delimited, Tab Delimited, Other User-defined delimiter, HTML table, XLS file, Insert Statements, SQL Loader, XML (Plain), or XML (with XSL). As you change formats, you may notice that additional options appear for those formats; for example, NULL text, Zip Resulting file(s), and file or clipboard destination.

Note that the data saved by the Save As command is not limited to the rows displayed in the data grid. All rows of data resulting from your query are saved to either the clipboard or a file (depending on which target you selected). Your saved data is sorted, filtered, excluded, and otherwise manipulated based on your display manipulations and the options you select in the Save Grid Contents window.

Procedure Editor

TOAD's Procedure Editor is designed to make the editing, compiling, and executing of stored programs as easy as possible. The Procedure Editor and the SQL Editor have many functions in common; the overlap between them includes both traditional editing and Oracle-centric editing functions. However, the Procedure Editor provides many specific features that facilitate the handling of different types of stored programs such as procedures, functions, packages, and triggers. These features include specialized navigation, entering and saving parameters, program execution, the use of the DBMS OUTPUT package, and so on. The Procedure Editor allows you to create new stored programs, work with existing stored programs, or work with script files.

You can access the Procedure Editor in two different ways. Either click on the "Procedure Editor" button on the TOAD Standard toolbar to open a New Procedure Edit window, or click on **Database → Procedure Editor**. In both cases, Procedure Editor opens an empty editor window.

Procedure Editor Options

Many of the options that TOAD allows you to customize have an impact on the Procedure Editor. These range from adding the owner when extracting source from the database to limiting TOAD to one Procedure Editor per database connection. This section summarizes the most important options and suggests possible customization.

The options discussed here are those we recommend you change; they are available from the **View → Options → Procedure Editor**.

In addition, many of the editing options discussed earlier for the SQL Editor also apply to the Procedure Editor. See the discussion of the **Right Mouse → Editing Options** and the **Edit → Editor Options** in the "SQL Editor" section. These options are common to all TOAD editors, so any changes to them are reflected in the SQL Editor, the Procedure Editor, and the Text Editor.

Enable compiling multiple objects from a single file
> This option is available from **View → Options → Procedure Editor**. You may want to set it (default is unchecked) if you will be working primarily from scripts. Although setting this option helps in compilation, it also disables the Debugger (see the "Debugger" section), so you will need to consider this tradeoff.

> If this option is active, three additional compile options display on the Procedure Edit toolbar:

Compile *to* the cursor position from the beginning of the editor.

Compile *from* the cursor position to the end of the editor.

Compile only the highlighted statement.

NOTE

Setting the *Enable compiling multiple objects from a single file* option disables the Debugger. Disabling the option enables the Debugger again.

Use "CREATE" instead of "CREATE OR REPLACE" when loading database objects

This option is available from **View → Options → Procedure Editor**. Consider whether it is more appropriate for your work environment to use CREATE instead of CREATE OR REPLACE (the default) when loading database objects.

Load packages into separate tabs when loading source from database

This option is available from **View → Options → Procedure Editor**. Consider the convenience of enabling load packages into separate tabs when loading source from a database.

StartUp Window per Connection

This option is available from **View → Options → StartUp**. If you anticipate spending much of your time in the Procedure Editor, consider changing the Procedure Editor to your default TOAD startup window. Remember to uncheck your previously defined startup option as TOAD will open all selected windows at startup.

Configuring the Procedure Editor

TOAD provides many options for configuring and customizing the Procedure Editor to meet your editing needs. The **Right Mouse → Procedure Editor Desktop** menu lists options to display or hide the Navigator panel, the Debug Output panel, and the Status toolbar. The various toolbars (Edit, Main Procedure Edit, and Debug) are customizable from this same menu.

Procedure Editor Display

The default Procedure Editor window is divided into two vertical panels; additional panels appear when necessary:

Navigation panel
> This panel always displays on the left. It shows the specification (spec) and body for the stored program that you are editing. (See the discussion later in this section for more details.)

Code-Editing panel
> This panel always displays on the right. It displays the code corresponding to the spec and body shown in the Navigation panel.

Errors panel
> This panel opens across the bottom of the Procedure Editor window when errors are encountered during compilation. The appropriate PLS or ORA error and its description display in this panel. At the same time, the line where the error was detected is highlighted in the Code-Editing panel. (See the later "Right Mouse › Compile" section for more information.)

Debug Output panel
> If you have the add-on TOAD Debugger module installed, a dockable Debug Output panel (with tabs for Break Points, Watches, Call Stack, and DBMS_

OUTPUT) displays in the lower right panel. (See the discussion in the "Debugger" section.)

The Navigation panel lets you view the procedure names and function names in a package, as well as navigate to the displayed spec and body code elements in the Code-Editing panel. The Navigation panel places your cursor at the beginning of any procedure or function displayed in the Code-Editing Panel when you click on its name.

The default display lists procedures and functions in the order in which they appear in your code. If you wish to sort them alphabetically, click on the Sort button on the Navigation panel toolbar. If you prefer to use keyboard keys to move through the Navigator panel, use:

- The up arrow (↑) or CTRL-PgUp to move *up* through the Navigator panel
- The down arrow (↓) or CTRL-PgDn to move *down* through the Navigator panel

Procedure Editor Menus and Toolbars

The Procedure Editor displays two toolbars, described in the following sections. In addition, a right mouse menu, also described here, is available from the Procedure Editor.

Procedure Edit toolbar

The Procedure Edit toolbar is the second toolbar displayed in the Procedure Editor. Commands for *Compile the current source*, *Check in/Check out from source control*, *Load source from existing object*, *Create new PL/SQL object*, and so on are displayed here. If you have the optional Debugger module installed, the Debug toolbar is displayed at the right end of the Procedure Edit toolbar.

Status toolbar

Once a stored program has been loaded or created, the Status toolbar displays the stored program's current valid/invalid status, the creation date, and the date last modified.

Procedure Editor → Right Mouse

The **Procedure Editor** → **Right Mouse** menu (shown in Figure 7) offers more than two dozen commands. Some commands are standard editing commands, and some you may recognize as duplications from the SQL Editor's right mouse menu. However, a number of commands, such as *Compile* and *Execute without Debugging*, are unique to this right mouse menu.

This section describes only those commands that may not be self-explanatory.

The Procedure Editor lets you work on several stored programs at one time; each is loaded on an individual labeled tab. Use the *New File/Tab* and *Close File/Tab* commands to govern these operations. These commands are available from the **Procedure Editor** → **Right Mouse** menu or by right-clicking on the appropriate tab. Note that the Procedure Editor can also be configured to load a package's spec and its body into separate tabs.

Populating the Procedure Editor

You can populate the Procedure Editor with existing stored programs from your Oracle instance or from script files. These can be accessed in a number of ways.

There are load options on the TOAD Menu toolbar. You can load files by selecting either **Tools** → **Import Source Files** or **File** → **Open**. There are various choices for loading from files or from existing sources in your Oracle database on the Procedure Editor toolbar. Files can be loaded using the:

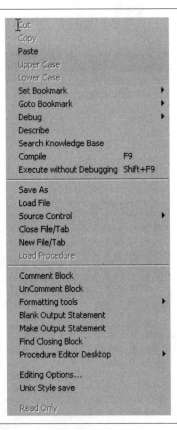

Figure 7. Procedure Editor right mouse menu

"Load File" button on the Procedure Edit toolbar

"Load Source from an existing object" button on the Procedure Edit toolbar

First select the appropriate schema/owner. Then select objects from groupings of any of the following: procedures, functions, complete packages, package specs, package bodies, complete types, type specs, type bodies, and all stored programs. A preview panel displays your code for review before loading it in the Procedure Editor.

You can load stored programs from the Schema Browser. From either the Procs or Triggers tab, highlight the desired stored program on the left Objects panel. Once the object is highlighted, select **Right Mouse** → **Load** in the Procedure Editor.

Procedure Editor Shortcut Keys

The Procedure Editor provides a set of shortcut keys that you can use instead of selecting options from the various editing menus. Table 2 lists all available keys.

NOTE

The list of shortcut keys in Table 2 is specific to the Procedure Editor's Code-Editing panel. There is a fair amount of shortcut key definition duplication among the SQL Editor, Procedure Editor, and Text Editor. However, there are also significant differences. For example, the shortcut F9 runs a command in the SQL Editor, but it compiles a stored program in the Procedure Editor.

Table 2. Procedure Editor shortcut keys

Shortcut key	Function
F1	Windows Help for current window
F2	Show/hide Errors panel
F4	Describe highlighted table, view, procedure, function, or package in pop-up window
F5	Set or delete breakpoint on the current line
CTRL-F5	Add watch at cursor

Table 2. Procedure Editor shortcut keys (continued)

Shortcut key	Function
F7	Trace into
F8	Step over
SHIFT-F8	Trace out
F9	Compile
SHIFT-F9	Execute without debugging
CTRL-F9	Set parameters
F10	Display right mouse menu
F11	Run (continue execution)
F12	Run to cursor position in Code-Editing panel
CTRL-ALT-B	Display breakpoints
CTRL-ALT-D	Display DBMS_OUTPUT
CTRL-ALT-E	Evaluate/modify
CTRL-ALT-S	Display call stack
CTRL-ALT-W	Display watches
CTRL-Pg Up	Move up in the Navigator tree
CTRL-Pg Dn	Move down in the Navigator tree
ALTL-Pg Up	Switch to the next tab to the left
ALTL-Pg Dn	Switch to the next tab to the right
CTRL-Mouse Click	Move to the selected package procedure

Using the Procedure Editor

The following sections describe various Procedure Editor commands and operations that may not be self-explanatory.

Customizable TOAD templates

When the TOAD Procedure Editor opens, it displays a blank, untitled tab for entering a new program from scratch. Alternately, you can load and manipulate source from a file or an existing program. You can also use the default TOAD templates for a new procedure, function, package, or trigger.

From the Procedure Edit toolbar, click on the "Create New PLSQL" button. This opens the New Procedure Create Options window, where you enter the new object name. Then select the appropriate object type (e.g., *procedure*) from the pull-down list.

All TOAD New Object Templates are stored as SQL files in the *TOAD\temps* folder. The default files are named *NEWFUNC.SQL, NEWPACK.SQL, NEWPROC.SQL,* and *NEWTRIG.SQL*. You can edit these files according to your local standards, or you can create your own template files and add them to the New Object Templates through **View → Options → Proc → Templates**.

Right Mouse → Blank Output Statement/Make Output Statement

TOAD provides a quick utility for creating DBMS_OUT-PUT.PUT_LINE statements. Selecting **Right Mouse → Blank Output Statement** creates a "DBMS_OUTPUT.PUT_LINE ('');" statement and copies it to the clipboard. After positioning your cursor at the appropriate location, select **Right Mouse → Paste** or CTRL-v to paste the output statement into the Procedure Editor.

In addition to creating blank output statements, TOAD can use the value of a variable that you enter to produce a complete output statement. Position your cursor on a variable name and select **Right Mouse → Make Output Statement**. The variable name is included in the statement that is created in the clipboard as follows:

```
DBMS_OUTPUT.PUT_LINE ( 'variable_name= ' || variable_name)
```

DBMS_OUPUT package

Before you execute code that generates output from Oracle's
DBMS_OUTPUT package, you need to open the TOAD
DBMS Output window and enable polling for output from
this package. From the TOAD Standard toolbar click on the
"Open a new DBMS Output window" button.

Once the window is displayed, verify that the settings are
appropriate for what you're planning to do. The first button
on the DBMS Output window toolbar toggles output polling
on and off. Then verify that you have set the DBMS Output
buffer to an appropriate size. When TOAD encounters a call
to DBMS_OUTPUT during stored program execution, that
output will be directed to this active DBMS Output window.
You may find it useful to set **Window → Tile Horizontal** to
allow you to view both the Procedure Editor and the DBMS
Output window at the same time.

Right Mouse → Find Closing Block

The **Right Mouse → Find Closing Block** function locates the
closing block for a highlighted "BEGIN" (TOAD searches for
an "END"), "IF" (TOAD searches for an "ENDIF"), or "(",

(TOAD searches for a ")". For example, highlight the BEGIN in question, and then select **Right Mouse → Find Closing Block**. The highlight moves to the corresponding END. Note that at this time, this function is unidirectional; it moves from BEGIN to END, not the other way.

Right Mouse → Compile

TOAD provides several launch points for compiling your program. You can click on the Compile button, the first button on the Procedure Edit toolbar. You can also select **Right Mouse → Compile** or press F9.

If errors occur during compilation, an Errors panel opens at the bottom of the Procedure Editor window with the appropriate PLS or ORA error and its description displayed. The line of code where the error was detected is also highlighted in the Code-Editing panel. Compilation stops at the first error that is encountered. Subsequent errors may be discovered after you've corrected the original error and restarted compilation. Sometimes Oracle returns more than one error when you compile a procedure. The Errors panel has arrows on its left side that let you browse through all of the errors returned for the last compile.

Call procedures, functions, and packages

There are several ways to call procedures, functions, and packages within TOAD:

- You can create and execute an anonymous block from the SQL Editor window. Note that a call to a stored procedure must be a full anonymous PL/SQL block (i.e., must have a BEGIN and END).

- You can execute a procedure, function, or package from the **Schema Browser → Procs** tab. Highlight the stored program name and then **Right Mouse → Execute Procedure**.

- If you have the Debugger option, select **Procedure Editor → Right Mouse → Execute** without debugging or use Shift-F9.

Text Editor

In addition to the SQL Editor and the Procedure Editor, TOAD provides a built-in Text Editor. The Text Editor is not Oracle-aware, but it does share the TOAD code templates, the SQL templates, and the basic code formatter with the SQL Editor.

You can open the Text Editor by clicking on the "Open a New Text Editor window" button on the TOAD Standard toolbar.

The Text Editor supports multiple open files; if multiple files are used, each displays on its own tab.

In addition to the TOAD Text Editor, you can use an offline text editor such as Microsoft Word if you wish. Support of an offline editor is helpful in organizations that require all documents to be composed with a particular text editor. This feature combines the power of the TOAD framework with the convenience of working with an editor you're familiar with.

SQL Modeler

TOAD's SQL Modeler provides a fast means for creating the framework of a SELECT, INSERT, UPDATE, or DELETE statement. You can select tables, views, or synonyms; join columns or select columns; and create the desired type of statement, all via point-and-click operations.

You can access the SQL Modeler from the TOAD Menu toolbar by selecting **Database → SQL Modeler** or from the TOAD Standard toolbar by clicking on the "Open a New SQL Modeler" button.

For a more complete discussion of the SQL Modeler, see the "SQL Modeler" chapter in the TOAD Help files.

Schema Browser

TOAD's Schema Browser is a convenient tool for reviewing the current status of a particular schema's Oracle objects. You can inspect an entire set of objects at one time (e.g., all tables in the database) or examine the in-depth details of one specific object (e.g., a constraint). The Schema Browser lets you enable, disable, alter, copy, drop, export, compile, and perform a variety of other actions on the objects you select. Note, however, that the current Oracle privileges of the logged-in user determine which actions you are allowed to perform. These privileges also affect your ability to display and alter objects owned by other schemas.

You can open the Schema Browser in several different ways. You can select the "Open a New Schema Browser window" button (the second button on the TOAD Standard toolbar).

Alternately, you can select **Database → Schema Browser** from the TOAD Menu toolbar. If you have designated the Schema Browser as the default startup window when TOAD connects to Oracle, the Schema Browser will open automatically at startup time. You can make Schema Browser your default window by setting it in **View → Options → StartUp** (see the discussion of Schema Browser options in a later section).

TOAD checks your Oracle version and displays or suppresses Schema Browser tabs (shown in Figure 8) according to the Oracle version to which you are connected. For instance, the Schema Browser does not attempt to report on policies or libraries when connected to an Oracle 7.x database (which doesn't support such objects).

NOTE

The Schema Browser typically handles one object at a time. In order to select more than one table, view, stored program, or other object simultaneously, select **View** → **Options** → **Schema Browser** → **Page 1** → **Allow multi-select on the left-hand lists**. Note that the multi-select option is not available on all Schema Browser tabs; you will have to manipulate certain types of objects one at a time. Also note that enabling this feature disables drag-and-drop for object names.

Schema Browser Display

The Schema Browser window is divided into two panels:

Objects panel
> The left panel shows the database objects you are inspecting.

Details panel
> The right panel shows the related details of the high-lighted object.

Both the Objects panel tabs and the Details panel tabs have (in most cases) their own toolbars and right mouse menus.

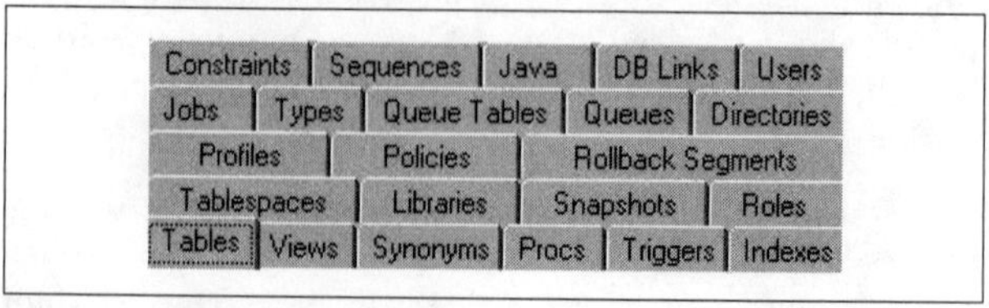

Figure 8. Schema Browser tabs

If you have the optional TOAD-DBA module enabled, the Schema Browser will have several additional tabs available, as shown in Figure 8.* These currently include Directories, Libraries, Policies, Profiles, Rollback Segments, Roles, Snapshots, Snapshot Logs, and Tablespaces. You can create, alter, modify, and drop these objects via the Schema Browser. (See the "TOAD Database Administration" section for more information about the TOAD-DBA module.)

Schema Browser Options

You may want to customize certain Schema Browser options to suit your work environment. Adjusting these options affects how quickly the Schema Browser can load, which tabs to load first, which users/schemas to omit, and so on. The options are available from **View** → **Options** → **Schema Browser** → **Page 1** and **View** → **Options** → **Schema Browser** → **Page 2**.

View → Options → Schema Browser → Page 1

Consider changing the following options:

Enable DROP-ALL Buttons
  Consider checking this option on (default is unchecked). You will have to determine how important it is to be able to drop database objects quickly. Note that this is the only item under **View** → **Options** that is not saved from session to session.

Limit data grids to [blank] number of rows
  You might want to specify a limit for the number of rows to be displayed in the data grid, especially if the database has very large tables or views. The default is *blank*, which will return all rows.

---

* More tabs are likely to be added as TOAD adds more Oracle features (e.g., dimensions).

Cache cursors used for queries (faster Browser but uses 12 cursors)

Consider checking or unchecking this option (default is checked). Caching makes the Schema Browser run faster. If you check this option, TOAD uses cursors when retrieving detail information to display in the Details panels to the right of the Schema Browser window. Usually, only the object name changes from query to query. Consequently, using cursors in which only the bind variable values change is much faster than forcing Oracle to reparse and re-execute different queries each time.

Automatically show filter dialog for filtered lists on Browser

You might want to check this option (default is unchecked) if you typically apply Schema Browser filters. If you enable this option, a filter dialog displays, allowing the user to enter filter criteria for tables; the Schema Browser opens with only the objects that meet the criteria.

View → Options → Schema Browser → Page 2

You may also want to change the following options:

Allow multi-select on the left-hand lists (disables drag-n-drop object names)

Consider enabling/disabling this option if you need to manipulate multiple objects at once.

User/Schema Lists

Select the display options most suitable for your environment. Decide if it's better to *Show all users* (the default), *Only show users that own objects,* or *Only show users that own objects excluding Synonyms.*

Tabbed Schema Browser

Unchecking this feature (default is checked) enables an alphabetical pull-down list in place of the left-side tabs in the Schema Browser.

View → Options → StartUp

You may want to set the Schema Browser to be your default startup window. You can do this by selecting **View → Options → StartUp** and selecting *Browser*. If you make this change, though, remember that the *SQL Window default startup* option does not automatically load all the objects for the logged-in schema when connecting to Oracle. On the other hand, the Schema Browser immediately loads all tables for the connecting schema when it is initiated. You can select multiple windows to open at startup.

Schema Browser Commands

Many of the Schema Browser commands are fairly self-explanatory. In the following sections, we briefly describe those that need to be explained.

Display/Hide/Rename

There are approximately two dozen tabs available for display on the left side (Objects panel) of the Schema Browser. You can configure these in various ways. The Schema Browser lets you hide the tabs you use infrequently. You can also adjust the order in which the tabs are displayed.

To configure the tabs, position your cursor over the tabs on the left, and right-mouse click. From the list displayed you can click on the tabs you want to display and click off the tabs you want to hide. You can reset these at any time.

To adjust the order, select the *Configure* option from the bottom of the tabs' right mouse menu. You can see the tabs displayed in Figure 9. The Tables object is fixed (locked) as the first tab displayed, but the Views, Users, and other types of objects can all be relocated.

You can also change the labels on the Objects panel tabs from the same window. The first column lists the object type, and the second column lists the name displayed on the

Figure 9. Schema Browser Objects panel tabs (Configure option)

tabs. You can change labels to suit you. For example, you might want to change the Procs label to Procs/Func/Pack (because procedures, functions, and packages are all displayed on this tab).

Review object status

The Schema Browser populates with objects owned by your logged-in TOAD user. From the Tables, Views, or Synonyms tab, click on the first object name in the list in the left panel to display objects of that type. The Schema Browser displays the total count for the tables, views, or synonyms in the lower left corner of the window. The details for the highlighted object display in the Details panel on the right side of the screen; details include the dates the object was created and updated, the data, the script for a table or the code for a function, and so on.

You need the appropriate Oracle privileges, permissions, and grants in order to view or manipulate objects in the Oracle database through the Schema Browser. An object will not display in the Schema Browser if your user is not allowed to access it.

Review relational integrity (entire schema)

The Constraints tab in the left Objects panel displays all the constraints owned by the displayed schema. Highlight the constraint to populate the Details tab on the right.

The Constraints toolbar, like all of the Schema Browser toolbars, lists actions that are appropriate for the objects being displayed. Thus, you are allowed to enable, disable, and drop individual constraints. You can also choose to enable and disable all constraints at one time.

You can click on the "Filter List of Constraints" button on the Constraints toolbar to enable the filter; this lets you display or hide SYS constraints, check constraints, unique constraints, and so on.

NOTE

Each tab on the Objects panel has its own toolbar. Many of the tabs have their own right mouse menus as well. If a tab does not have a unique right mouse menu, TOAD displays the Tabs/Configure menu.

Review relational integrity (table)

When you highlight a table on the Tables tab or the Synonyms tab, the Constraints tab in the right Details panel lists only those constraints that are on that particular table. These may include primary and foreign keys, as well as SYS constraints. The **Table → Constraints** toolbar is basically the same as the toolbar on the Objects panel Constraints tab. However, two additional buttons ("Add Constraint on this Table" and "Drop All Constraints") are available on this toolbar.

To review referential integrity for a table, highlight the table name and then click on the Referential tab in the Details panel. The Schema Browser displays the tables that reference, or are referenced by, the highlighted table. You can continue to click through the list of tables on the left to view their Referential information.

The Used By tab checks to see if procedures, views, snapshots, etc., use the highlighted table. This tab usually takes longer to populate than the Referential tab as TOAD checks for cross-schema references.

Check for invalid objects

The Procs tab (shown in Figure 10) displays the stored programs in the Oracle database.

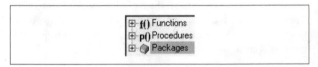

Figure 10. Schema Browser Procs tab

Expand the list of procedures, functions, or packages (note that triggers have their own tab). If any of the displayed stored programs are invalid, they are flagged with an X.

"Compile Invalid Objects" is the first button on the Procs toolbar. Click on this button to compile all of the invalid objects for the selected schema. The Schema Browser prompts with a "Do you want to continue?" message. You might want to consider reviewing the individual errors via the Errors tab on the right instead of issuing a blanket compile of all invalid objects. The right mouse menu lists commands to compile the stored programs one at a time or load them into the Procedure Editor.

You can also generate a printed, HTML, Adobe Acrobat (PDF), RTF, Excel, or *.jpg* formatted report showing all or selected invalid objects in the database. See the discussion in the later "TOAD Database Administration" section.

Modify existing Oracle objects

Many of the Schema Browser panels have buttons or right mouse menu options that allow you to modify a selected object. For example, the Tables tab has options to *Add Columns*, *Drop Columns*, *Create Indexes*, *Rename Table*, and so on. All of these selections launch templates with the appropriate radio buttons, pull-down lists, etc., to generate storage parameters and do whatever else is needed to build the SQL required to make the change.

NOTE

Always check the "Show SQL" button when making changes in any of the modify object windows. This way, you can examine the SQL that TOAD is building as you make your entries and pull-down menu selections in the object templates.

Review/add table and column comments

The Schema Browser window provides an easy method to review existing table and/or column comments and to create new comments.

Highlight the table to be reviewed in the left Objects panel and then select the Columns tab in the right Details panel. Click on the Comments button on the Columns tab toolbar.

Select the comments type from the drop-down list (shown in Figure 11). The existing comments will display, and you can type new comments in the lower half of the Column tab's Details panel.

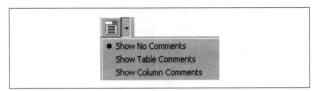

Figure 11. Schema Browser Columns tab/Comments list

After editing and before closing the Schema Browser window, be sure to select a different table for the comment editing to be sent to the database. Changes to comments are automatically posted to the database when you browse through another table.

NOTE

You can add table and column comments in a more traditional manner by directly altering the table. Select **View → Tables → Right Mouse → Alter Table**. The Alter Table window has a Comment column at the right end of the column grid. A separate tab lets you enter table comments. Clicking the OK button executes the generated SQL. A report on table comments by selected schema or all schemas is available from **View → Reports → Tables**.

Create new Oracle objects

Nearly all the Schema Browser Object tabs have a "Create New" button on their toolbars, as well as a **Right Mouse → Create New** function. Using the Create templates helps remind you of options that may have been omitted or forgotten when working in a script format. Create New is a particularly good feature for learning how to create new Oracle object types and work with new Oracle features, such as partitioning. The fill-in-the-blank boxes, pull-down lists, and other items make the task of building the correct SQL faster and easier. As with modifying Oracle objects (see the "Modify existing Oracle objects" section), always check the "Show SQL" button when creating objects with TOAD.

Java

The Schema Browser allows you to display the code for Java sources, Java classes, and Java resources in your Oracle8*i* or higher databases.

The Java tab toolbar has buttons to compile a Java object and drop a Java object. **Java → Right Mouse** also lets you print, save to the clipboard, or save to a file. Note that the Drop All option is not available for Java objects, so the Schema Browser is limited to dropping Java objects one at a time.

Sequences

Schema Browser → Sequences displays all of the sequences for the selected schema. When you highlight a sequence, the parameters and grants display in the Details panel. Both the **Schema Browser → Sequences** toolbar and the **Schema Browser → Sequences → Right Mouse** menu contain options to create the sequence, alter the sequence, add or change privileges, drop the selected sequence, and drop all sequences. **Sequences → Right Mouse** also has an option to reset the sequence.

SQL Tuning

TOAD provides a number of tools for identifying and tuning poorly running SQL—for example, statements that are CPU-intensive or I/O-intensive. These tools include:

- Explain Plans that show how Oracle executes a statement
- Several commands for reviewing statistics after statement execution, including Explain Current SQL, SGA/Trace Optimization, and Kill/Trace Session
- TOAD's optional SQL Tuning Lab module and the Oracle Probe API.

Explain Plans

EXPLAIN PLAN is an Oracle command that analyzes a SQL statement for performance without actually executing the statement. The purpose of this command is to determine before execution the plan that Oracle will follow when optimizing and executing a SQL statement. The results of the EXPLAIN PLAN display the order in which Oracle will search/join the tables, the types of access that will be employed (indexed search or full table scan), and the names of indexes that will be used. The display is read from the deepest indentation out vertically.

Explain Plan in the SQL Editor

 In the SQL Editor, you can generate an EXPLAIN PLAN command before executing a valid SQL statement by clicking on the "Run Explain Plan for current statement" button (the ambulance) on the SQL Edit toolbar. You can also press CTRL-E to generate the plan.

The generated plan displays on the Explain Plan tab available from the Results panel. If you wish, you can display this information from the right mouse menu. The *Run Explain Plan for current statement* command is also available in the SQL Modeler.

TOAD expects to find an Explain Plan table with columns matching the most recent specification from Oracle. If you get Invalid Column errors when executing the EXPLAIN PLAN command, check in the *TOADPREP.SQL* script for the columns you may be missing. The TOAD Explain Plan table is backward-compatible with earlier Oracle releases.

You can set the name of the Explain Plan table in the **View** → **Options** → **Oracle** window. Adjust the information in the dialog and enter your Explain Plan table name and the username for the Explain Plan.

Previous Explain Plan results

TOAD stores previously generated Explain Plans for review and comparison. You can access these from **View → Explain Plan** or by clicking on the "Show Previous Explain Plan Results" button (the ambulance button with the blue line above it) on the TOAD Standard toolbar.

The resulting multi-paneled Explain Plan window displays previously generated plans. You can compare the generated plans for variations of the same queries, different queries, and so on. This window does not have any editing capabilities, so if you decide to make changes to the displayed SQL statement, you must do so in the SQL Editor. Once you've made these changes, you can generate a new Explain Plan while in the SQL Editor and then return to the Explain Plan window and click the Refresh button to update the display.

You may occasionally need to perform some maintenance to clear Explain Plan results that are no longer needed. Select the obsolete Explain Plan results and click Clear.

Before you can use the Previous Explain Plan Results feature, you must go to **View → Options → Oracle** and turn on the *Save previous Explain Plan results (requires TOAD tables)* option. You will need to create the necessary tables and their related objects by executing either the *TOADPREP.SQL* or the *NOTOAD.SQL* script. Both scripts are located in the *TOAD\temps* folder.

SQL Tuning Commands

The following sections describe a variety of TOAD commands used to review statistics and tune SQL statement execution.

AutoTrace

TOAD's AutoTrace feature lets you review resource usage for a particular query in the SQL Editor. AutoTrace is a mini-version of Oracle's SQL Trace (described in the next section). Unlike TOAD's Run Explain Plan for current statement command, which can be generated without executing a statement, AutoTrace requires that the statement be executed in order to generate its results.

AutoTrace displays information such as Recursive Calls, Physical Reads, Consistent Gets, Index Scans, etc. The results are displayed in the AutoTrace tab of the Results panel.

If AutoTrace is not enabled when you click the AutoTrace button in the Results panel, TOAD prompts you to enable it. You can enable or disable AutoTrace from **SQL Editor** → **Right Mouse** → **AutoTrace**. Once enabled, AutoTrace remains enabled until you disable or until the TOAD session is terminated.

NOTE

Because AutoTrace forces a read of all data resulting from your query, you may notice that it adds overhead to Oracle.

SQL Trace (TKPROF)

SQL Trace (TKPROF) is a server-side Oracle trace utility that captures CPU, I/O, and resource usage during statement execution. SQL Trace is a much more complete utility than AutoTrace. The output file is created on your Oracle server in the directory specified in the *USER_DUMP_DEST* parameter of your *INIT.ORA* file (containing Oracle initialization parameters). You can view this file from **Tools** → **TKPROF Interface**.

The TKPROF wizard-driven interface prompts you for the trace file(s) you want to view, lets you choose sort options and data elements to view, and then displays the results in a separate window.

To enable the TKPROF interface, select **View → Options → Executables**. If the path for your TKPROF executable is not identified, click on the flashlight icon to have TOAD locate the path for you.

SGA Trace Optimization

You can use the **Tools → SGA Trace Optimization** command to view information about SQL statements that have been executed and the resources they used. Whereas Auto Trace and TKPROF information is specific to a single statement, SGA Trace Optimization displays statistics from multiple SQL statements currently present in Oracle's SGA (System Global Area).

Go to **Tools → SGA Trace Optimization** to open the SGA Trace window. You can set several options from this screen in order to search for SQL statements. The default settings are for ALL Statements for ALL Users, but you can click on the corresponding drop-down box and choose another option to change these choices. You can limit the selection to a single statement type (e.g., SELECT statements, UPDATE statements, anonymous PL/SQL, etc.) or to a specific user. You can also enter a text string in the SQL Search Text box to limit the rows returned to statements containing that text string.

Click on the "Refresh the List of Statements" button to retrieve the most resource-intensive SQL from the SGA. This returns all of the queries that match your criteria. The screen is divided into two parts:

- The query results grid on the top half of the screen shows the query that was executed and the associated resources used (memory, disk reads, loads, etc.).
- The bottom half of the screen displays the full SQL statement, execution statistics from the Oracle shared pool, and the Explain Plan for the query.

When necessary, you can pass a SQL statement into the SQL Editor from the SGA Trace window. Highlight the desired statement, then click on the "Load selected statement in a SQL Editor" button on the SGA Trace toolbar.

This toolbar also contains a button to "Flush the SGA." Your Oracle privileges dictate your logged-in user's ability to use this function.

NOTE

Tools → SGA Trace Optimization requires access to a number of Oracle V$ objects. For a current listing of the Oracle access required to utilize this feature, go to **Help** → **Contents**. From the Table of Contents, select **TOAD Basics** → **V$ Tables Required**.

Kill/Trace Session

The **DBA** → **Kill/Trace Session** option, like **Tools** → **SGA Trace Optimization**, requires access to a number of Oracle V$ objects. The Kill/Trace window displays session information on the use of locks, blocking locks, and rollback segments. The Access tab lists objects by each user in the current session. You can also review the current statement and open cursors for each user. When necessary, you can selectively kill sessions using the *Kill the selected session* command from the Kill/Trace toolbar. Your ability to execute a kill session is governed by the logged-in user's Oracle privileges.

Selecting *Start trace for this session* from the Kill/Trace toolbar enables traces for selected user sessions. Selecting *End trace for this session* disables traces for these sessions.

Oracle Probe API

TOAD uses the Oracle Probe API to collect performance data on PL/SQL applications. To use this feature, you must first verify that you have the DBMS_PROFILER package (created by Oracle's *PROFLOAD.SQL* script). Then use the TOAD user (created by *TOADPREP.SQL*) to run *TOADPROFILER.SQL*.

Toggle **Database → PL/SQL Profiling** on and then execute your stored program. The Profiler prompts you to name each run (execution). As each run completes, the Profiler Analysis window displays performance data for each line of code. Because this information is stored in database tables, you will be able to run ad hoc queries and customize your own reports.

Additional Tuning

TOAD provides an add-on module, the SQL Tuning Lab, that lets you perform additional SQL statement tuning. When necessary, you can pass a SQL statement from the SQL Editor or the Procedure Editor directly into the SQL Tuning Lab. See the description in the "SQL Tuning Lab" section.

Debugger

TOAD provides an optional PL/SQL debugging module that provides full debugging capabilities for stored programs (e.g., procedures, functions, triggers, package procedures, and package functions). This module lets you do things such as the following:

- Perform line-by-line debugging and error trapping
- Set breakpoints and watches; with these, you can monitor specific values inside the procedure, function, or package, as well as the passing/changing of variables passed to the program

This section provides a variety of tips for using the Debugger with the Procedure Editor. Much more detailed information is available in the TOAD Help files and in the Debugging chapter in the *TOAD User's Guide*.

NOTE

TOAD's Debugger utilizes the Oracle Probe API (v2.0 or later). Make sure that software is installed and that Oracle's DBMS_DEBUG package exists under the SYS schema. Each TOAD Debugger user requires Execute privilege on DBMS_DEBUG.

Also note that the TOAD Debugger can handle only a single object per tab. You can compile multiple objects from a single file, but you cannot debug a file containing multiple PL/SQL objects.

Setting Debugger Options

You can customize the Debugger to suit the way you work. Debugger options are available from **View → Options → Debugging**. The following are the options we recommend you consider changing:

Save proc parameters between sessions
    You may want to check this option on so the parameters used during execution are saved between sessions. The parameters are stored in your local *TOADParams.ini* file for reuse the next time you execute the same stored program.

Transaction Control
    Three buttons in the Transaction Control box provide Commit, Rollback, and Prompt choices. Selecting Commit or Rollback appends an Oracle COMMIT or ROLLBACK statement to the anonymous block created by the TOAD Debugger prior to executing stored programs (see the "Setting Parameters" section for more details). If you select Prompt (the default), TOAD will ask if you want to "Commit changes to debug session?" each time you execute or debug code in the Debugger.

Default to "Compile with Debug"
> If this option is checked (default is unchecked), the "Toggle compiling with Debug" button on the TOAD Standard toolbar will be in the on position when each Procedure Editor session begins.

Compile Dependencies
> Three buttons in the Compile Dependencies box provide Yes (the default), No, and Prompt choices. Consider which option is suitable for your environment.

Date format for watches
> Select the appropriate date format used for watches in your environment (default is DD_MON-YY). This format will be the NLS_DATE_FORMAT for the Debugger session.

Debugger Menus and Toolbar

You can select Debugger options from the TOAD Debug menu (available from the TOAD Menu toolbar), the Debugger toolbar, or the **Procedure Editor → Right Mouse → Debug** menu.

The menus are slightly different. The TOAD Debug menu (shown in Figure 12) provides one additional execution option, Run to Cursor. The menu also has controls for breakpoints and watches.

The Debug toolbar (shown in Figure 13) has one option not available from the Debug menu: the button on the far right, "Compile referenced objects with Debug." Otherwise, the icons match the commands on the Debug menu.

The **Procedure Editor → Right Mouse → Debug** menu (shown in Figure 14) is an abbreviated but handy version of the main Debug menu and Debug toolbar.

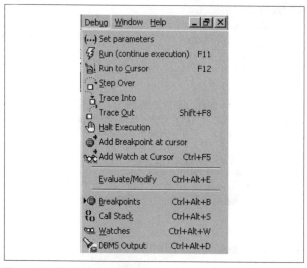

Figure 12. TOAD Debug menu

Figure 13. TOAD Debug toolbar

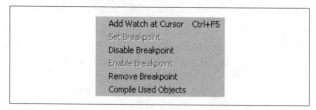

Figure 14. Procedure Editor right mouse Debug menu

Debugger Display

TOAD's Debugger includes all of the features of the Procedure Editor's display (see the earlier section, "Procedure

Editor Display"). In addition, the Debugger has a dockable window with four tabs: Breakpoints, Watches, DBMS Output, and Call Stack. As usual in TOAD, the tabs have unique interior toolbars and right mouse menus.

Breakpoints

If you have set a breakpoint on a line, stored program execution will stop before the code on that line is executed. You can set a breakpoint by positioning the cursor on the appropriate line of code and clicking F5. Alternately, you can set a breakpoint menu by clicking in the editor's gutter to the left of the appropriate line of code. Breakpoints can also be set from either of the Debug menus.

You can set conditional breakpoints from **Right Mouse** → **Edit breakpoint** from the Breakpoint tab. With a conditional breakpoint, execution stops only when a defined condition is met.

You can also display breakpoints from the **Debugger** → **Breakpoints** tab. That tab has an interior toolbar and a right mouse menu with additional breakpoint options.

Watches

If you place a watch on a variable, you can display and evaluate its value during stored program execution. To set a watch, position the cursor on the variable and set the watch from the Debug menu, the Debugger toolbar, or the **Procedure Editor** → **Right Mouse** → **Debug** menu. Alternately, position the cursor on the appropriate line of code and press CTRL-F5.

Watches are displayed in the **Debugger** → **Watches** tab. The tab has an interior toolbar and a right mouse menu providing additional watch options.

Once you've set a watch, you should review the Watch Properties regularly from the Watches tab by selecting **Right Mouse** → **Edit Watches**. The Watch Properties dialog provides an additional option, *Break on a Value Change*, which lets the Debugger use breakpoints more effectively.

Watch variables can be either simple (i.e., scalar) variables or records. When a record is watched, the hover-over will show the values for all of its component variables. When placed in the watch window, records display as a tree of values, with one tree node for each component variable.

DBMS Output tab

Any output generated by calls to the DBMS_OUTPUT package (discussed in the "Procedure Editor" section) during a debugging session is displayed in the **Debugger → DBMS Output** tab. Output is released from the DBMS_OUTPUT buffer after execution has been halted or completed. In nested procedure calls, all procedures must run to completion before any DBMS_OUTPUT results are displayed.

Call Stack window

The Call Stack window displays the chain of procedures and functions as they are called. The line number references the code line number in the Procedure Editor window. The Call Stack window is active only during execution.

Setting Parameters

When you begin a debugging session, you may want to consider the impact of setting values for IN and IN/OUT parameters as opposed to running your program with NULL values. You can set values from **Debug → Set parameters** or by selecting the "Set Parameters" button on the Debug toolbar.

(...)

This opens the Set Parameters dialog. The Debugger displays the parameter name, data type, and IN/OUT mode. TOAD now builds an anonymous block to execute the stored program. The block displays in the lower half of the Set Parameters window. As you enter values, the anonymous block is updated. Alternately, you can directly edit the generated anonymous block.

TOAD assigns NULL values to any IN/OUT parameters whose values you do not specify.

NOTE

When you make changes to the anonymous block, the "Rebuild Code" button at the bottom of the window become active. Use Rebuild Code to resynchronize the anonymous block with the values entered in the grid.

Executing a Stored Program from the Debugger

You can run a stored program by selecting **Debug → Run**, by pressing F11, or by clicking the "Run the current procedure with Debug Info" button on the Debug toolbar. (This button is the same lightning bolt displayed on the **Schema Browser → Procs** toolbar.)

There are additional execution options for executing the code one line at a time, for stepping over or tracing into procedure or function calls, and for tracing out of a called procedure to return to the caller on both the TOAD Debug menu and the Debugger toolbar.

Executing a Stored Program Without Debugging

TOAD allows you to execute a stored program without running it through the Debugger. Select **Procedure Editor → Right Mouse → Execute Without Debugging**. The Execute Without Debugging function opens the Set Parameters dialog and creates the necessary anonymous block (described in the "Setting Parameters" section).

After Debugging

When you complete a debugging session, there is one final step you need to perform in order to clean up the Debugger's symbol table. Toggle off the "Toggle compiling with debug" button and compile your stored program once more. It will now recompile without the debug symbol tables.

Other TOAD Menus

This section describes the basics of several TOAD menus not yet discussed: the Tools menu, the Create menu, and the Help menu.

The Tools Menu

The TOAD Tools menu (shown in Figure 15) provides many functions that you are likely to recognize—for example, Estimate Table Size and Analyze All Tables. The menu also includes some functions that are unique to TOAD—for example, viewing foreign key-related data via the Master Detail Browser, Object Search for objects such as column names or object names, or searching source code in the database. This section discusses only the options that need explanation.

Tools → Master Detail Browser

The Master Detail Browser command lets you view related table data in a database in which foreign keys link the tables. Start by selecting the desired schema. Then select a parent table. Once the parent table has been selected, only related tables will be available from the related table. As you select each table, the first four rows of data are displayed in the grid. As you click through the rows of data in the parent table, the related rows of data display in the child table's data grid. The Master/Detail Browser can display one parent and up to four related tables.

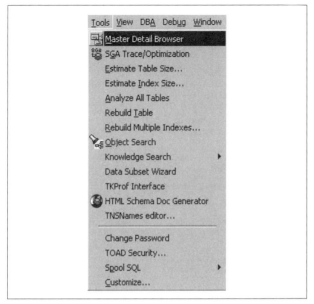

Figure 15. TOAD Tools menu

You can add a row to a grid by pressing the Insert key or the down arrow while on the last record in the grid. This function also allows you to edit records. There is also a limited right mouse menu available; options include Print Grid, Save As, Copy Row, and Record Count.

Tools → Data Subset Wizard

The Data Subset Wizard lets you copy a specified percentage of data from one schema to another and maintain referential integrity. For instance, you can use this function to copy 10% of the data from a production server, thus creating a meaningful subset of real-world data for testing and development.

The Data Subset Wizard generates a commented script that includes creating the target tables, truncating the tables, manipulating storage, and so on. That script can be saved to a file or immediately loaded into TOAD's SQL Editor. The script includes all parent tables, as well as tables with no constraints and tables that have foreign key constraints. The rows copied are those whose parent rows have been copied into the parent tables.

If the schemas reside on different instances, TOAD uses a database link to the source schema while the script is run on the target instance.

The Data Subset Wizard inserts data into your destination tables via INSERT SELECT statements, such as the one shown here. Tables containing columns of data type LONG will not be inserted.

```
insert /*+ PARALLEL(Dest, 4) APPEND */
  into QUEST_DEV.OW_CUSTOMERS Dest
  select /*+ FULL(SRC1) PARALLEL(SRC1, 4) */
  from   QUEST_PROD.OW_CUSTOMERS SRC1
  where rownum <= (select
  /*+ FULL(SRC2) PARALLEL(SRC2, 4) */
    greatest(10, ceil((10/100) * count(*)))
    from QUEST_PROD.OW_CUSTOMERS SRC2);
```

Tools → Object Search

The Object Search command allows you to search for an object in the database. TOAD matches the text string entered in the Search For dialog box with source code or Oracle objects that contain that text string. You can specify the desired object name as an object, a column name, a trigger column, a trigger source, an index column, or a constraint column. (Note that you cannot use this option to search the data itself.)

When searching by object name, you can qualify the text string by specifying the following options:

- Case sensitivity
- Exact match

- Starts with text
- Text occurs anywhere

Note that "exact match," "starts with text," and "text occurs anywhere" do not apply to a source code search.

You can limit your search to a single selected user or expand it to all users. You can also choose to include or exclude SYS and SYSTEM objects from the search.

Search results are displayed with the object name and its associated object type, parent, and owner. You can search the displayed grid by clicking on the column header.

A **Right Mouse** → **Describe** command is available directly from the object name. The right mouse menu also has an option to load the highlighted source object into the Procedure Editor.

Tools → TNSNames editor

The *TNSNAMES.ORA* file is a text file used by Oracle Net to resolve net service names when local naming is used. The TNSNames editor command provides an easy method for viewing and editing such files. You can view and edit a single TNSNames file or work with two TNSNames files simultaneously. In the latter case, your TNSNames files will display side-by-side in two adjacent panels, making it easy to visually compare the two. An alphabetical Sort button is available on the TNSNames Editor toolbar; sorting makes it easier to navigate through your defined services.

Both the left and right panels have both upper and lower panels. Once a TNSNames file has been loaded, your services are displayed in the upper panel, and the details for the highlighted service are displayed in the lower panel. The lower panel has two tabs: the first displays the name and details of a highlighted service, while the second displays your entire TNSNames file. When you have two TNSNames files open, you can copy services between them. The editor also lets you create new service entries.

When you elect to modify a service, you can add or edit a service from either the toolbar or from **Right Mouse → Add Service** and **Right Mouse → Edit Service**. These options bring up an appropriate dialog window covering both basic and advanced service entries.

To drop a service, you can select **Right Mouse → Delete Service,** click the Delete button on the toolbar, or press the Delete key on your keyboard. TOAD will immediately drop the highlighted service from the TNSNames editor.

NOTE

TOAD will not update the displayed TNSNames file(s) until you click on the OK button at the bottom of the screen or click on the Save button on the TNSNames window toolbar. Also note that the TNSNames editor will make a backup of the original file in the same folder.

Tools → Spool SQL

Select the Spool SQL function if you are concerned about the commands that TOAD is sending to Oracle. Examining these commands should provide insight into how TOAD is gathering statistics, altering objects, and so on.

When you enable spooling, you need to select the appropriate menu option. Determine whether TOAD should send the SQL to a window (**Tools → Spool SQL → To Screen**) as each command is executed, or send the SQL to the *DEBUG.SQL* file in the *TOAD\temps* folder for later review (**Tools → Spool SQL → To File**). Each offers advantages and disadvantages.

Tools → Spool SQL → To Screen
This command immediately starts spooling TOAD commands to a Debug Output window. The commands display in the order in which they are executed, and the

next command will not display or execute until you either close the window or click off the *Spool SQL To Screen* option in the lower left corner. Sending commands to the screen, rather than to a file, is often beneficial in that it lets you study each command as TOAD issues it.

Tools → Spool SQL → To File

This command appends its output to the *DEBUG.SQL* file in the *TOAD\temps* folder. The spooled entries are clearly timestamped, and execution is continuous. You may regard both the timestamping and the continuous execution as advantages over the **Spool SQL → To Screen** option. But there is also a disadvantage to file spooling. Because TOAD appends to the *DEBUG.SQL* file whenever this option is selected, the file can become quite large if you don't judiciously maintain it.

NOTE

Despite the fact that these options send commands to the Debug Output window and the *DEBUG.SQL* file, they are not true debugging options. For information about the actual TOAD Debugger, see the "Debugger" section earlier in this book.

The Create Menu

TOAD's Create menu (shown in Figure 16) provides the ability to easily and accurately create many different types of Oracle database objects. The Create menu shown here lists all of the supported object types; this menu contains a number of options available only when you have installed the optional TOAD-DBA module (in this case, on an Oracle8*i* or later database).

The following options are available only if the TOAD-DBA module is enabled: Directory, Library, Policy, Profile, Roles,

Figure 16. TOAD Create menu

Rollback Segment, Snapshot/M(aterialized)-View,[*] Snapshot Log, and Tablespace.

The Create menu functions are also available via the Schema Browser's object tabs. For example, you can launch the job's Create dialog either from **Create → Job** or from **Schema Browser → Jobs → Create Jobs**.

The following sections describe two representative Create commands.

---

[*] Create Materialized View and Create Snapshot are combined into a single option.

Create → Sequence

The **Create → Sequence** dialog lets you create new sequences in the TOAD user's schema. The Create Sequence dialog prompts you to enter the following: a sequence name, a "start with" value, minimum and maximum values, and "increment by" values; it also accepts cycle, number to cache, and order information. Once the dialog is complete, Execute and Cancel are the only options.

NOTE

The generated SQL can be captured or viewed during execution via the **Tools → Spool SQL → To Screen** or the **Tools → Spool SQL → To File** option. (These options are discussed in the "Tools › Spool SQL" section.)

Create → Table

The **Create → Table** dialog prompts you to enter a number of table options. You can define the new table as standard, global temporary, index organized, clustered, or queue (used by Oracle Advanced Queuing). TOAD displays the appropriate tabs for the type of table being created; examples include Columns, Organization, Partitions, Comment, or Queue. Each tab has a specific set of options. Where appropriate, pull-down menus are also available.

For example, when Advanced Queuing is selected as the table type, tabs for Queue Tables and Organization appear. **Queue Tables → Payload Type → Object** displays schema names and objects, while **Organization → Tablespaces** displays the list of tablespaces.

The Help Menu

If you have a problem or question, you can get help in a number of ways via TOAD's Help menu:

TOAD Help files
> The Help files in TOAD do a very good job of documenting current features, new features, and enhancements. The first menu item available from the Help menu (Contents) opens the TOAD Help files. Context-sensitive help is available from anywhere in TOAD by clicking F1. The right mouse menu in the Help menu lets you add your own annotations to any displayed help topic.

Support
> The Support option available from the Help menu gives you the choice of connecting to web-based support or creating email to *support@quest.com*.

Join Mailing Lists
> The Join Mailing Lists option available from the Help menu gives you the opportunity to participate in the TOAD group at *http://www.yahoo.com* or in the TOAD beta program.

TOAD Database Administration

TOAD provides a powerful, but easy-to-use interface for managing the many ongoing tasks associated with Oracle database administration. Use TOAD in conjunction with routine Oracle maintenance activities (e.g., monitoring user activity, space usage, etc.), as well as with less routine activities like creating new databases.

You can access database administration functions from various locations in TOAD, including the Schema Browser window and the Create, Database, Tools, and View menus. A number of these functions are located on TOAD's DBA menu, and several require that the add-on TOAD-DBA module be installed. In the following sections, we'll label each entry according to the command's location in TOAD.

Using the TOAD-DBA Module

The TOAD-DBA module is an optional, add-on configuration of TOAD features designed especially for use by the Oracle DBA. It adds extended functionality to TOAD's Schema Browser, Create menu, and DBA menu as follows:

Schema Browser
> Displays additional tabs for items such as Directories, Libraries, Policies, Profiles, Rollback Segments, Roles, Snapshots, Snapshot Logs, and Tablespaces

Create menu
> Also provides the ability to create the items added to the Schema Browser

DBA menu
> Displays the following additional tabs: Database Monitor, Instance Manager, Unix Monitor, Unix Job Scheduler, Windows Registry Parms, Unix Kernel Parms, Database Health Check, Top Session Finder, Oracle Parameters, National Language Support Parameters, Tablespaces Map, Control Files, Pinned Code, New (Create) Database Wizard, Redo Log Manager, Log Switch Frequency Map, Log Miner, Export and Import Utility Wizards, SQL Loader Interface, Generate Schema Script, and Compare Schemas

Monitoring the Database

The following sections describe a variety of TOAD commands you can use to monitor your Oracle database and watch for space problems.

DBA → Instance Manager

Use the Instance Manager to verify the status of the nodes, listeners, and databases for your monitored instances. The Instance Manager window can either use a previous TOAD login to the target databases or permit a test connection for any valid login. You can also start, stop, or alter a selected database from the Instance Manager. You can set Instance Manager options via **View → Options → Instance Manager**.

Check alert logs

You need to check the Oracle alert logs periodically for new entries. If your alert log files are located on Windows servers, you can access the alert logs from either the SQL Editor window or the Text Editor. Your alert log location is specified by the BACKGROUND_DUMP_DEST parameter in your *INIT.ORA* file.

If your alert logs are located on Unix servers, use **File → Network Utilities → Telnet** to view the file on the server.

Schema Browser → Tablespaces and DBA → Tablespaces

To obtain a detailed, multi-tabbed view of all of your tablespace statistics, select either **Schema Browser → Tablespaces** or **DBA → Tablespaces**. The two approaches are not quite equivalent:

- Both approaches let you create or modify tablespaces, and create or modify datafiles. Both provide Datafiles, Free Space, Objects, and Fragmentation tabs.

- Only **Schema Browser → Tablespaces** has an Extents tab and a Properties tab.
- Only **DBA → Tablespaces** has a Space History tab and an IO History tab.

The major difference between the two approaches is that **Schema Browser → Tablespaces** details one tablespace at a time, while **DBA → Tablespaces** generally displays information on all tablespaces in a grid.

You can obtain the following information:

Datafiles

This tab displays the tablespaces and their associated datafiles with a complete path description, online/offline status, and extent information. You can sort the information in the displayed grid by clicking on any column header.

Free Space (in KB)

This tab displays the number of blocks and the minimum, average, maximum, and total amount of free space for each tablespace in grid format. As with the Datafiles display, you can sort the data in the grid by clicking on any column header.

Objects

This tab is populated after you select a tablespace name from the drop-down menu. Details on all the objects, including owner, name, and object type, are displayed in a sortable grid format along with each object's extent information; that information includes the extent, next extent, number of extents, maximum extents, and size of the extents in bytes and MB.

NOTE

The use of **DBA → Extents**, which provides extent information by selected schema rather than by tablespace, is discussed in the next section.

Fragmentation

This tab displays fragmentation information by tablespace. The grid includes columns showing total blocks, empty blocks, number of fragments (pieces), size of fragments, and number of usable fragments.

Use the **View** → **Reports** → **Other Reports** → **Tablespaces Near Capacity report** to identify all tablespaces that are at least 90% full, and that do not have Autoextend enabled.

DBA → Extents

You can identify spacebound objects by checking their defined Next Extent values. TOAD's **DBA** → **Extents** command opens the View Extents window, which displays the datafile extents information by selected schema.

The default display is All Objects, but you can restrict the selection by choosing only to display tables, indexes, rollback segments, or clusters. After choosing All Objects or the selected object types, select the owner from the pull-down list. Once you click on the Go button on the toolbar, TOAD displays the following columns in the grid: Object Name, Type, Tablespace, Total Size (in KB), Initial Extent, Next Extent, (existing) Extents, and Max Extents. Click on the column header to apply an ascending or descending sort.

We recommend that you print and review this extent information regularly to keep up with growth trends in your database.

NOTE

DBA → **Extents** requires access to DBA views in order to select owners from the drop-down list. Otherwise, TOAD uses SYS.USER_EXTENTS to populate the View Extents window with the logged-in user's information.

Schema Browser → Rollback Segments

You can verify the current status for each rollback segment by selecting the Rollback Segments command from the Schema Browser. Toolbar options allow you to create a rollback segment, alter it, take it offline, place it online, and drop it. You can select these tabs:

Info
> This tab displays storage parameters for the rollback segment, with details ranging from the owner to a fully qualified datafile name.

Stats
> This tab displays values for active sessions, writes, gets, waits, high water mark, extents, shrinks, and wraps.

DBA → Identify Space Deficits

From **DBA → Identify Space Deficits** you can examine the tables in a tablespace to identify those that don't have sufficient free space to allocate their next extent. If you want to resolve this problem on the tablespace level, use the "Alter Tablespace" button at the lower left of the screen. This will launch an Alter Tablespace, Alter Datafile, and Create Datafile dialog.

DBA → Tablespaces → Space History

From **DBA → Tablespaces → Space History** you can display an historical graph of database usage. This command also provides options to forecast anticipated space usage either by tablespace or datafile. (Note that Space History does not display in the Schema Browser.)

DBA → Tablespaces → I/O History

From **DBA → Tablespaces → I/O History** you can display a datafile's I/O history, including physical and block-level reads/writes and times. (Note that I/O History does not display in the Schema Browser.)

NOTE

Some of the tablespace management commands require use of TOAD's Space Manager tables. You must log in as the modified TOAD user and then click the "Create Space Manager Tables" button on either the Space History tab or the I/O History tab.

The modified TOAD schema must have the privileges to create and alter jobs, as well as to create and drop its own tables and procedures. This schema must also have SELECT access on Oracle's DBA_TABLESPACES, DBA_DATA_FILES, DBA_FREE_SPACE, and V_$FILESTAT views in order to complete this install.

DBA → New Database

DBA → New Database opens a wizard-style interface for DBAs to use when creating a new Oracle database. This interface is helpful in constructing your new *INIT.ORA* file, assigning tablespaces across available hard drives (or volumes), and then building either the database or the scripts to perform the build. You can use the wizard to create new databases for any version of Oracle and for both Windows and Unix target server platforms.

DBA → Pinned Code

DBA → Pinned Code lets you pin PL/SQL objects in the SGA and prevent Oracle from overwriting that code. The judicious pinning of PL/SQL objects improves Oracle performance.

This command displays the DBA Pinned Code window, which contains two panels:

Upper panel
    This panel displays PL/SQL objects currently cached in the SGA. These can be pinned in the SGA by first highlighting the desired objects and then clicking on the padlock icon on the DBA Pinned Code toolbar.

Lower panel

This panel lists, by schema, all of the procedures, functions, and packages that exist in the database. In addition to pinning objects currently in the SGA cache, you can choose to pin these PL/SQL objects into the SGA. Use the same process described for other objects.

You can unpin objects by following the same process.

NOTE

The DBA Pinned Code window Auto-Refreshes by default. You might want to slow or pause the refresh operation while you are selecting objects for pinning.

Tools → Rebuild Multiple Indexes

If you need to maintain one or more indexes as a result of growth or fragmentation, use the **Tools → Rebuild Multiple Indexes** function. In addition to generating the rebuild script, this function analyzes all or selected indexes. Many user-defined options are also available. Following the analysis, the program will recommend indexes for rebuilding. Note that program recommendations are based on user-supplied conditions.

DBA → Oracle Parameters

You can view Oracle's *INIT.ORA* file from TOAD. Selecting **DBA → Oracle Parameters** opens a window that displays your *INIT.ORA* parameters in a grid format with the following column headings:

Option

Displays the parameter name.

Settings

Shows the current value specified for that parameter.

Default
> Indicates whether the current parameter value is set to the default value.

Description
> Provides a brief description of the parameter's function.

Session Modifiable, System Modifiable
> Both columns display "Yes" or "No," indicating the parameter's modifiable status.

You can print an instance's list of initialization parameters by pressing the Print icon on the Oracle Parameters window's toolbar.

DBA → Oracle Parameters (change modifiable parameters)

If you have the TOAD-DBA module installed, you can modify many of the Oracle initialization parameters in the *INIT. ORA* file from within TOAD. (Users who do not have the TOAD-DBA module are limited to viewing the *INIT.ORA* file via TOAD.)

To modify a parameter, select **DBA → Oracle Parameters** and then double-click on the desired parameter in the displayed grid. If the parameter you want to change is either system-modifiable or session-modifiable, a pop-up dialog box opens. Enter the new value into that dialog box.

NOTE

If a parameter is both session-modifiable *and* system-modifiable, TOAD will modify it at the system level. Be aware that session-level parameters are modified for the current session only. Changed system-modifiable parameters do not persist after a database reboot.

Check database statistics

You can use TOAD to review common Oracle tuning points. These include cache hit ratios, latch contention, and memory management. You'll find the following reports helpful:

View Reports → Other Reports → User Hit Ratio
> This report includes information on consistent gets, block gets, hit ratios, and physical reads ordered by user.

User DBA → Health Check
> Use this report to examine the overall operating conditions for your databases.

DBA → Server Statistics
> Use this report to examine event wait and timeout statistics. It displays detailed CPU and Oracle statistics by individual session. The Instance Summary groups all of the individual session information together.

NOTE

You can allow the Server Statistics Sessions report to refresh on command or set it to Auto-Refresh at a user-defined interval. Exercise judgment whenever using an Auto-Refresh–enabled window in TOAD; be aware that Auto-Refresh will continue to run when this window is in the background.

DBA → Log Miner (review logs)

TOAD provides a wizard format interface for using Oracle's Log Miner packages. DBMS_LOGMNR and DBMS_LOGMNR_D provide access to online/offline and archived Oracle redo log information.

Select **DBA → Log Miner** and specify the location of the dictionary and whether you want to create a new one. Use Browse to select the files. If your database is on a Unix server, an FTP dialog box displays. Review the SCN range and date range settings, Oracle9*i* options, and so on. Then select the information to be displayed in the Log Miner Interface grid.

Check for objects that break the rules

One way to keep close watch on database activity is to check for any objects that break the rules. Use the following options:

Schema Browser → Tables → Constraints
    Set the Tables filter so this command will search in all schemas; this way, all tables will display.

Schema Browser → Constraints
    Use this command to review constraints by schema.

Schema Browser → Tablespace → Objects
    Use this command to review and discover which objects reside in the source tablespace. You can sort object names to allow you to check naming-convention consistency, as well as owner and object type.

View → Reports → Table Reports → Table Constraints
    This report generates a detailed report on constraints including status, type, delete rule, etc.

View → Reports
    Various **View → Reports** reports, the Schema Browser, and the DBA menu can all be used to verify that naming conventions and storage conventions have been followed.

Use DBA → Compare Schemas

Use this command to ensure that schemas look identical across environments (especially across development, test, and production environments). **DBA → Compare Schemas** generates a detailed comparison report. This command lets you create a synchronization script to bring the schemas into uniformity. In order to run this script, TOAD requires an Oracle Net connection, and Oracle requires the appropriate

---

privileges. The Compare Schemas function will work for schemas on the same instance or on different instances. Note that this function does not examine data.

NOTE

If you discover major differences between the compared schemas, you should seriously consider using **DBA →
Generate Schema Script** to generate a complete migration script to resolve the differences rather than using the **DBA → Compare Schemas** synchronization script.

Use DBA → Unix Monitor

Use **DBA → Unix Monitor** to check on CPU usage, process queues, and disk I/O on the Oracle server. The Unix Monitor supports Linux, Sun OS 5.7/5.8, HP-UX 11.0, IBM AIX, and TRU64 (the Disk I/O graph is not supported for TRU64).

Database reporting

TOAD gives you various tools that allow you to document many areas of your database; for example:

Tools → HTML Schema Doc Generator
Produces a customizable report. The report can range from a single schema to multiple schemas. It provides options for extensive customization for formatting, object inclusion/exclusion, etc. The fact that the completed Schema Doc report is in HTML format is often an advantage.

View → Reports
You can generate many views from **View → Reports**, including reports on tables, views, invalid objects, user resource usage, and non-system objects in the SYSTEM tablespace. These reports can be formatted in HTML, Adobe Acrobat, Rich Text, Microsoft Excel, or as a Graphic (*.jpg*) file.

Performing User Administration

TOAD provides a number of tools that can help perform user administration. These tools allow you to create users, roles, profiles, storage, grants, and quotas. You can also use TOAD to monitor users and users' objects and tablespaces.

You can select any of the following:

Database → Schema Browser → Users
Allows you to review and modify a user's assigned roles, privileges, and storage. Users can also be locked/unlocked, modified, and cloned from the Users tab toolbar and the right mouse menu.

View → Session Info
Displays Oracle session privileges, granted table privileges, roles, and role privileges for the currently logged-in user.

View → Reports → Other Reports → User Resource Usage Reports
Reports the Oracle resource name, providing a value for each resource (e.g.,"Recursive Calls 3, 295").

DBA → Kill/Trace Session
Displays active and inactive users with extensive details about their sessions. Information includes open cursors, lock waits, physical reads, and other information that may affect role and profile administration.

DBA → Top Session Finder
Shows which Oracle sessions are using the most resources on the database, according to weighted criteria that you set up.

Database → Privileges
Brings up a window for administering the users and roles in the database and viewing the set of users with various system privileges.

Performing Database Export/Import

TOAD provides a number of Oracle Export/Import options. These can be found in the appropriate Schema Browser tabs, Grid menu, SQL Editor Data tab right mouse menu, Database menu, and DBA menu. Many of the options on the Database menu are also available in the Schema Browser. Note, however, that the export options vary; the Schema Browser is single-object-oriented, while the **Database →** **Export** functions can handle multiple objects.

Database → Export → Export Table Scripts

Use this command to export the table scripts for a designated schema/owner. When you select the schema/owner name from the drop-down menu at the top of the screen, the table names for that schema/owner display in a long list; you can change that list to a columnar display by using the arrows at the lower left of the screen. You can select a single table, multiple tables, or all tables (via the "Select All" button at the bottom of the screen).

After you have completed your selection, click on the OK button. This opens a Table Script Creation window containing Options and Output tabs:

Options
> From this tab, make the appropriate choices for the script to be generated. You can include a DROP statement, indexes, tablespace information, constraints, grants, triggers, synonyms, etc.

Output
> From this tab, direct the output to the clipboard, to a single file, or to separate files for each table according to your defined path.

Database → Export → Grants

The Grants command follows a similar but simpler format for exporting the grants on all objects for a specified user. You can limit the export to only included grants issued by the selected schema. You can also direct the output to the clipboard or to a single designated file.

Database → Export → Table Data

The Table Data command exports the data for a single table or for all tables for a designated schema/owner. From the Options tab you can exclude null columns, include the schema/owner name in the INSERT statements, and direct the output to a singe file or to a separate file for each table. As with the **Database → Export → Export Table Scripts** option, when separate files are created, TOAD uses the table name as the file name.

Schema Browser → Tables → Export Data

The Data Export function available from the Schema Browser window is slightly different from the **Database → Export → Data Export** function. In the Schema Browser you are limited to exporting data from one table at a time. Right-click on a table name in the Tables tab and select Export Data. The Schema Browser export has options to export to a clipboard and an optional WHERE clause for filtering the data. You can also select particular columns to export and choose how often to insert COMMIT statements.

Database → Export → Source Code

The Source Code command exports the code for your selected schema's stored programs as SQL script files. The Source Code Export window includes selection options for choosing all the objects for a designated schema. You can also limit the selection to source code for all programs of a type; for example, all packages, all procedures, all functions,

---

all triggers, or all views. You also can select from the options *Create one file for all objects* or *Each object to a separate file*

If you choose *Group objects in the following files*, TOAD will create separate files for all procedures, all triggers, and so on.

If you select a single object type, an additional tab opens, allowing you to choose specific objects to include or exclude from the export. If you select all objects, tabs for selecting and unselecting individual stored programs do not display.

Database → Export → Table as Flat File

This command creates a flat file. By definition, a flat file is a file that does not contain TAB characters or comma characters (,) between values. A flat file also requires the creation of a companion Specifications file, which defines the table name, table owner, how many lines in the output file will be covered by a single record of data, the columns of data, the line they will appear on, the starting column, and the length of each column of data. This command handles all the details of creating both the flat file and the Specifications file.

From the Options tab in the Flat File Export From Table window, select the schema and table to export. Select the target, which can be the clipboard or a specified *.dat* file. Next, click on the "Generate Columns" button to finish setting up the Specifications file and then click on Execute.

Database → Export → Synonyms

The Synonyms command exports synonyms to a file. You can export public synonyms for objects owned by the selected schema or limit the selection to synonyms owned by a single schema. The generated script will contain either the CREATE SYNONYM or DROP SYNONYM command. If you want to add a DROP statement to the script, just click on the option *Include DROP statement*.

Database → Export → Sequences

The Sequences command exports all the sequences for a selected schema/owner to either a file or the Windows clipboard. You also have the option to include a DROP statement.

Database → Import → Source Files

This is the companion command for **Database → Export → Source Code**. It is designed to import, parse, and execute source code for stored programs in the form of SQL script files for procedures, functions, packages, triggers, and views. This command expects to find one object per file.

The Source Import window has a series of six buttons along the top of the window:

Add

> Use this button to access the Open window. From here you can select or multi-select the needed SQL files.

Remove

> Conversely, you can use the Remove button to eliminate a previously selected file from the Source Import window.

Parse Files

> Use this button to parse the highlighted file. This action checks the script's syntax. The object type, object name, and its valid/invalid status are displayed along the same row as the path and filename information. The object will be listed as INVALID if it is invalid or does not exist. If the object code fails to parse, the Errors panel at the bottom of the screen displays the appropriate PLS error number along with its description.

Load in Editor

> Selecting this command or double-clicking on the displayed filename loads the selected file into the Procedure Editor. There you can view, modify, and save changes to

your displayed source code. As with any TOAD editor, you can save your changes to a new file or your original file. The object will not be created until you compile or execute the script.

Execute

This button completes the import by creating the objects in each script. Each script will be executed, and the results of the import will be displayed in the Status column. If errors are reported you can click through the list and review the related details in the Errors panel at the bottom of the window.

Cancel

This button terminates the operation and closes the Import Source window

DBA → Export/Import Utility Wizards

The **DBA** → **Export Utility Wizard** and the **DBA** → **Export Import Wizard** handle tables, users, tablespaces, or an entire database. The **DBA** → **Export Utility Wizard** provides a more extensive export facility than the **Database** → **Export** and **Database** → **Import** functions described earlier. They cover a greater range of database objects in a straightforward wizard fashion. The Export/Import Utility Wizards also utilize parameter and log files and provide the ability to zip the export files even if the user does not have a zip utility.

Additional TOAD Modules

As TOAD has changed from freeware to a commercial product, it has become a modularized product as well. Add-on modules for TOAD now include the following:

- Debugger
- SQL Tuning Lab
- Knowledge Xpert for Oracle Administration

- Knowledge Xpert for PL/SQL Development
- TOAD-DBA Module
- The TOAD Suite (includes DataFactory™, Benchmark Factory® for Oracle, and QDesigner™ Physical Architect)

All are described briefly in the following sections. Consult the TOAD Help files for more information.

Debugger

The add-on Debugger module provides extensive PL/SQL debugging facilities for stored programs (procedures, functions, triggers, package procedures, and package functions). For information, see the "Debugger" section earlier in the book.

SQL Tuning Lab

TOAD's optional SQL Tuning Lab module lets you tune SQL statements. You can take a SQL statement and generate optional queries and schema changes to help optimize the performance of the statement. The tuning module also allows you to test different query scenarios and do a side-by-side comparison of the results to determine which query will perform best in your environment.

Knowledge Xperts

Two Knowledge Xpert programs are available for use in TOAD: the Knowledge Xpert for Oracle Administration and the Knowledge Xpert for PL/SQL Development. Both Xpert modules provide current Oracle documentation, sample scripts, coding guides for Oracle7, Oracle8, Oracle8i, and Oracle9i syntax, and so on.

TOAD-DBA Module

The add-on TOAD-DBA module activates additional menu items in TOAD's Create menu, DBA menu, and Schema Browser. It also adds additional functionality to existing menu items; for example, with TOAD-DBA installed, the Import/Export Utility Wizards include the SQL*Loader interface. For more information, see the "TOAD Database Administration" section earlier in the book.

The TOAD Suite

The TOAD Suite is a set of products including the complete TOAD program and several add-on modules: DataFactory™, Benchmark Factory® for Oracle, and QDesigner™ Physical Architect. This complete development suite provides all the tools necessary to design, develop, test, and manage your database.

DataFactory™

DataFactory™ is a data generator that allows developers and QA personnel to easily populate test databases with millions of rows of meaningful, syntactically correct test data. This add-on module reads a database schema and displays database objects such as tables and columns; users can then point, click, and specifically define how to populate the table.

Benchmark Factory® for Oracle

Benchmark Factory® for Oracle helps prevent unplanned downtime and slow performance by load-testing your system's limits using either industry-standard benchmarks or your own specified/captured transactional criteria before you go live with an Internet site, database, email system, or file servers.

QDesigner™ Physical Architect

QDesigner™ Physical Architect is a database design and application tool that combines object-oriented, conceptual, and physical data object–modeling capabilities in a single, integrated environment. This add-on module has an intuitive user interface and provides support for more than 30 popular DBMSs.

Index

We'd like to hear your suggestions for improving our indexes. Send email to
index@oreilly.com.